You Must Always be Good

Science and Behavior Books, Inc.
Palo Alto, California 94306

Library of Congress Card Number 76-15452

ISBN 0-8314-0053-6

Dedicated to a better understanding of the most helpless and dependent creatures in this world: little people—children.

Anneliese Ude-Pestel

The author wishes to thank Susanne Pestel for her sensitive translation and Peggy Granger for her fine editing and her deep understanding of this book from the very beginning.

Anneliese Ude-Pestel

Contents

Betty's Pictures

1. Strangled dead man
2. Dismembered dead man
3. Ghost with two child skeletons
4. Crocodiles with child skeletons
5. Vulture with children
6. "Large ghost bites into child's blood"
7. Girl's head with mice and spiders
8. Broken dolls
9. Embryo
10. Indian girl on the cross
11. Portrait of a woman
12. Rat in the mind
13. Sun with evil fingers
14. Gorgonian head
15. Dinosaur
16. Mute school-girl
17. Two dogs with corner store
18. Giant crocodile
19. Female dog
20. Girl with penis—Ghost in the bathroom
21. Birth and dancing death
22. Witches
23. Heart—Doctor (Arzt)
24. Cow in the meadow
25. A heart for Mommy ("Dear Mommy, I am very happy")
26. Dancing girl

Preface

In this book a child speaks to us about her fear and suffering. What her words cannot say, she expresses with pictures—her way of freeing herself from emotional pressure. To the viewer these deeply moving drawings offer an insight into the depths of the unconscious.

Betty is the story of a child who gradually fought her way out of her inner prison and emotional isolation, and found the way into a normal life. Her progress, during nearly two years of therapy, proceeded in such minutely small steps that it often appeared to be simply a marking of time or even a regression. However, Betty's remarkable development in this period comes into full view when we consider the dramatic changes she herself brought about. These changes are vividly illustrated in the first and last pictures reproduced in this book: the "Crucified" and the "Dancing girl."

These two pictures mark the beginning and the resolution of Betty's long struggle in which her wish for life eventually won over her wish for death; and in which she had to overcome severe fears of being persecuted and abandoned and even the fear of splitting off from herself. Out of hate and despair grew love, and thus the way was cleared for her development into a social being.

Due to the severe psychic disturbances of this child, a precise report was written up immediately after each session. Although I had no plans for future publication of the material at the time, these notes made it possible for me to give a faithful rendering of the dialogue between the child and therapist as well as a clear picture of the therapeutic process as a whole. For the sake of uniformity, repetitions have been omitted and the story greatly condensed. However, no words are used other than those originally spoken by Betty and her parents.

To Betty's parents who generously permitted the publication of this work, I owe special thanks. Without Annemarie Sänger, to whom I owe my training, this book would not have been written. I am also deeply indebted to Mr. Scheffler, Heidelberg, for his readiness at all times to discuss the therapeutic problems which arose during this difficult case.

Hamburg, Germany
December, 1974

Anneliese Ude—Pestel

*INTRODUCTION TO "BETTY: A Journal of
Child Play-Therapy"*
by Anneliese Ude-Pestel

To become an adult, a prized, elevated position,
we struggle to leave childhood behind us. Yet, as
child therapists, we expect to go backwards, to
descend in time, to play with our child patients,
and yet to understand fully as we mature adults
believe we must in order to help our patients. This
is not only a difficult task, it is sometimes impossi-
ble, and often painful. Inexperienced child therapists will walk many by-paths or make circuitous
detours to prevent the full array of childhood fears,
monsters and ghosts from appearing in the treatment room. As a child therapist Mrs. Ude-Pestel
is a full and mature adult, experienced, skillful,
and brave. She traverses with her child-patient
Betty the complete range of feelings—from thor-
ough despair and sadness to pleasure and ecstatic
happiness, and the more ordinary feelings of everyday life.

She describes for us a full course of treatment
from the early exploratory sessions with both
parents, the initial sessions with the child, up to
and including termination of treatment. This is
most useful since many clinical descriptions of child
therapy are of vignettes, interesting aspects of a

particular treatment, often only a portion of the treatment process and only infrequently include termination.

Early in the history of adult treatment, dreams were referred to by Freud as the "royal road to the unconscious." In child treatment, play and drawings are most important roads to the unconscious. In the preface the author mentions the "fear of suffering" that is expressed by the pictures. The non-word, non-adult expressions in play and in drawings are very important in child treatment and so difficult for adult therapists to comprehend. In this case the collection made by the father of this child's drawings prior to treatment is unusual and most informative. These pre-treatment drawings were produced by Betty, collected, dated, and annotated by the father, who also noted what Betty had to say about these ghosts and skulls. The drawings that accompany the treatment are an integral part of it and provide a unique opportunity to experience and learn more about the unconscious development of children.

The early history reported coherently by the parents, is filled with signs of difficulty. The mother describes poignantly being told of the death of her step-mother while still in "childbed" immediately after the birth of Betty. She experienced severe post-partum depression and could not breast feed her baby. The mother knew that often she went to the baby for comfort rather than being able to mother her child. The early toilet training history which began at 7 months indicates some of the origin of the child's excruciatingly painful constipation as a baby. This was accompanied by the development of persistent thumb sucking and stubbornness. Thumb sucking was "stopped" at four when the maid "broke" her of it.

Early Phase of Treatment

The description by Mrs. Ude-Pestel of her introduction of the parents to the process of treatment and to the therapy room is one that should be noted by both experienced and inexperienced therapists. The first sessions with the child illustrate clearly a sensitive and careful induction into the therapeutic process that facilitates the building of a therapeutic alliance. Mrs. Ude-Pestel describes swinging together, making milk, and yet in the course of these comforting activities, inviting her patient to venture into her fearsome inner world. The almost overwhelming anxiety of this child is illustrated clearly in Betty's early descriptions of rats grubbing and gnawing. Her pictures of ghosts, monsters and skeletons and crocodiles show the horrendous internal world that interferes with the daily functioning of this child. Because Betty's dream world is too frightening, she says, "I don't even want to sleep anymore." Fairy tales are used to aid the therapeutic process: Mrs. Ude-Pestel encourages Betty, "That you must find out for yourself, just like in the fairy tales. In them there are good and wicked fairies. The wicked fairies cast a spell on you, and the good fairies help free you from that spell." Betty replies, "I believe you are a good fairy . . . but sometimes it's the witches in fairy tales that cast spells on you." "Yes, that's right," Mrs. Ude-Pestel continues, "and then one must be very brave and walk through a large forest and overcome many dangers before one can get free of the spell." (Pg.27) Further on in treatment, Mrs. Ude-Pestel makes up fairy tales and even later on, Betty makes up her own self-initiated fairy tales. This sequence of fairy tales provides an excellent description of changes that occur during the therapeutic process.

Psychotherapy requires venturing into the world of internal unknown dangers. This exploration of chaos and confusion must be accompanied by access to and successful return to the safety of conscious reality. In the early phase of treatment when the patient was still possessed by her fears and fantasies, Mrs. Ude-Pestel describes a session in which her guidance and the return to reality after a venture into the morass of the unconscious, is illustrated: Betty was concerned with "bogs . . . and then the corpses stay way down there forever." The therapist replied, "Yes, there are bogs, but there are firm paths which lead across the bogs and when one follows these, one doesn't sink away." Immediately after this she turned to her patient and said, "Where did you see a bog?" And Betty returned to reality and discussed a visit to a museum. The therapist aided Betty in moving from her fear of being swallowed up, as expressed in picture 13, to return to the present day world. Such illustrations and lessons occur throughout treatment but they are particularly important in early phases when the development of the therapeutic alliance is so crucial for treatment to even be able to begin.

The use of drawings before treatment by this child in order to both express and control her anxieties has been mentioned. The father made a collection of these child's drawings which he brought to the initial sessions with the therapist. On p.47 the therapist utilizes drawings to pursue treatment further: "I sat down to draw, busying myself with a sketch pad and colored pencils. Maybe Betty would seize the opportunity to draw and bring out her unconscious problem." Betty responds, and we see a drawing of a sun with evil fingers. The therapist speaks casually to her as Betty is totally engrossed in her drawing. "She could give no verbal expression to it." The expression, however, in the drawing again pushes treatment further and in this instance allows us to see into her unconscious. Drawing and play are expressions in and of themselves. As adults we seem to feel that words must accompany or explain these expressions. The unconscious is not only timeless, but also places no particular premium on words. The expression of conflicts, feelings, and other instinctual derivatives is as useful in drawing and play as it is in words. We as adults seem to treasure words but the unconscious does not.

Middle Phase of Treatment

The establishment of trust developed in the therapeutic alliance of the early phase allows more difficult feelings and issues to emerge. In this phase of treatment with children issues of aggression often take the form of direct physical attack on the therapist. Mrs. Ude-Pestel describes such a session in which, well protected, she sets limit on the attack but does not turn away or totally prohibit these expressions. The full use of words instead of blows requires adulthood. Some adults never achieve this state but a child, particularly those with immaturities and difficulties in early development, may even require encouragement in the expression of aggression.

Mrs. Ude-Pestel worked with important people in the child's environment, particularly teacher and parents. In one session, after talking with Betty's teacher about her classroom performance, the drawing of a girl whose mouth is blotted out by large black circles appears. It is indeed Betty herself, the mute girl in her class. The black circles over the mouth symbolize not only her inability to speak in school, but also the dark and confused expressions that Betty feels she will give if she does speak. The therapist is aided in her understanding of this picture by her previous communications with the teacher.

The therapist describes gentle attention to the body. It is done without over-emphasis, but is included rather than omitted. The use of the body in play becomes an opportunity for discovery in a session in which wood shavings are imaginatively tossed in the air. This play is transformed almost magically by the therapist into discovery of body parts. In general, attention to the non-verbal aspects of treatment—elements such as silences and tensions—are aspects of treatment which might be said to be "in the air." They are felt, often not spoken of, but are as elemental as body parts. They are integral and crucial parts of any treatment, but particularly in child treatment. In another middle session, the oft–experienced desire by therapists to speed up the therapeutic process by pushing for change on the part of the patient is described. Mrs. Ude-Pestel gives specific "didactic" or educational advice. The response of the child is to turn her head away. This is a poignant and direct communication of an experience which child therapists often have. In an endeavor to rescue these children, therapists want them to change and to "get better." But "significant changes do not come from outside, but from within . . . dispensing formulas are meaningless to the child. Communication breaks down and the child withdraws." (Pg. 87) Later in treatment, a lovely fairy tale is made up by Betty, which concludes with, "When the buds of the water lily open, a pretty girl will come out." Betty expresses her understanding of readiness to emerge in this fairy tale. This occurs after considerable working and re-working in the middle phase of treatment.

Later Phases of Treatment

Some of the intricacies and progressions of the later phases of treatment are described. It is most important for a therapist to encompass other parts of the child's life as the recovering patient broadens her world to include others. Previously Betty's world had room only for ghosts, monsters, and fears. Now there is space for friends, animals, and ice skating. Mrs. Ude-Pestel includes a friend, Lilly, dolls and even her rabbit, Munchy. The flexibility and pleasure of these encounters is well described. In a late session a piece of play equipment provides a treatment summary. The therapist muses after a session looking at a cardboard box that had been part of treatment from the beginning and says, "First you were a cradle, maybe even the womb which Betty wanted to go back to. You had to be completely dark and quiet inside, and all she wanted was to be cradled gently back and forth in you . . . Then you were turned into a pirate ship with a death banner . . . and today you are a house, her house, her first house with an open door!" Indeed, this description of play material speaks clearly for itself, of the transition from closed off darkness to a self, possessing an open door and flowers.

In the termination phase of treatment, the patient leads and announces her readiness. The therapist's response to the request that she miss a session in order to go with a friend to a new activity is not regarded as resistance, but rather as appropriate to her psychological state and age. The earlier physical attacks as expressions of aggression have been transformed into games with rules in which one's opponent can be beaten. The therapist joins in joyously with latency age games with rules involving the intricacies of winning and losing.

In the drawings at this stage of treatment there is a contented cow grazing and a big heart with many little hearts. And finally, the self portrait of a dancing girl in a blue polka dotted dress who is happy. The therapist comments, "It was easy for her to leave." And yet, at the end, the therapist does not say as in books of fairy tales, "and they all lived happily ever after." as is our universal childhood wish. Rather, there is a reminder that though earlier periods have been revived and worked through, there are many potentially difficult times ahead in the course of the complicated process of growing up.

In this description the flavor of the multi-colored and varied activities of the child therapist are described with delight and detail. They have included potty play, the employment of cooking, swinging, and the many ways that are needed both to establish and pursue therapeutic alliance through the many vicissitudes of treatment. It will certainly be useful for adult therapists to read this description of work with children, perhaps even more so than for child therapists.

There may not be complete agreement with all the interpretations that are made. However controversial theoretical constructions are, certain elements of Betty's early history are not disputable. Mother's depression is described and confirmed and Betty's early childhood behavior is well described. From here on, including early intra-psychic development, all is construction. Fortunately, the child's unconscious has no set theory. There are some readers who will quibble or disagree completely with one theoretical explanation or another of the author. Particularly, the first moment of life has produced many explanations and disputes. The state of the infant and the question of the "will to live" at the moment of birth is open to considerable debate. The issue of life versus death and whether there is a desire to return to the womb at that moment is a matter that will probably remain unresolved. Those of different theoretical persuasions and moods will have different explanations. Whether or not the birth step should feel liberating is likewise an issue. However, good therapists and good therapy persevere in spite of these conflicts of theoretical orientation, and it probably makes little difference in what acutally happens in treatment.

In conclusion, this book probably will be read mostly by child therapists—"play-people." Beginning therapists who are frightened and confused will be reassured by reading an entire treatment at the time they are only experiencing beginnings. Others more experienced will read with interest, disagree, or mumble a bit as they enjoy the many details of a rich and varied total treatment process.

And perhaps there will be some adventuresome "grown-up" therapists who, turning away briefly from words and thoughts will experience, if only vicariously, many colors from black and purple in the pre-treatment and early drawings, as they turn to brown and eventually to sky blue and bright red. This child, Betty, went from black fear, monsters and ghosts to happy hearts and the regained pleasures of childhood. Mrs. Ude-Pestel has provided us with a rich experience, and many children and therapists I believe will benefit from this one case. Thank you.

Joan J. Zilbach, M.D.
Child Psychiatrist and Psychoanalyst
Director of Family Therapy and Research
Judge Baker Guidance Center
Boston, Massachusetts

1

"Whatever is the matter with Betty?"

Betty was barely six years old; yet already she was suffering from within herself as well as from the little world around her: her father and mother, her two-year-old brother, Sebastian, and the live-in babysitter, Lisa. However, they, in their turn, suffered because of Betty.

"Whatever is the matter with Betty?" her mother asked me in our first conversation. "This child tears at my nerves, exhausts my patience, and drains me of my last strength. Not even at night will she let me rest. She wants to lie between her parents. Lately she has been curling up in front of our bedroom door because I have forbidden her to come in.

"During the day she makes terrible scenes over nothing, throws herself on the ground in fits of rage, screams, and beats her head violently on the floor, as if she wanted to hurt herself. She tears out her hair, pulls off her clothes and wants to run around naked, because she feels too hot. She hates her little brother, strikes out at him uncontrollably, so that one has to protect him.

"She is also unkind to her dolls. She does not

1

play with them, but presses out their eyes and disfigures them.

"Betty rejects every act of tenderness on my part. She does not want to give or accept any love. She has no feeling. We often ask ourselves: 'Is this child still normal?'"

How much must have taken place for a mother to ask such a distressing question?

There was a moment of silence between us. My eyes wandered to a large box which the father had brought along and had placed before him. "These are all Betty's drawings," he explained, "which you have asked me to bring. There are about fifteen hundred of them. I had already made a collection of them, dated them, and occasionally I have noted at the bottom what Betty said about them. I imagine it must be interesting for you," he continued, "to try to come to a deeper understanding of Betty with the help of these drawings."

Out of this gigantic collection of drawings I pulled out one which differed from the others; it was rolled up to a thick scroll. The first figure to appear was an enormous skull staring at me from its hollow eyes. To this skull Betty had glued eleven pieces of drawing paper colored in red, forming, as it were, the body, so that the whole spectre had a length of twelve feet.

Together we looked at this ghost unrolled before us. Stood upright, it would not fit in my living room.

"It can give you the creeps," said the mother. And the father observed that Betty had a special liking for painting such ghosts and skulls of which there were dozens in the box.

We pulled out more pictures: a skeleton in diving-goggles, which seemed to be sinking away into deep water. Or next a strangled dead man (picture 1), or a dead man with his chopped-off red limbs scattered about (picture 2).

Next I came upon a ghostly looking giant's head with two black child skeletons dangling from his ears (picture 3). Again, two jet-black, frightening eyes stared out of the face with its broad, eerie grin. The neat row of numbers written on the monster's teeth intensified the unreal, demonic quality of this picture.

Many similar pictures followed. For instance, again child skeletons were hanged on a dark scaffold (picture 4). They were surrounded by seven floating crocodiles, and above them an enormous ghost with black, hollow eyes blocked every possible escape.

A solid black, overdimensional vulture dominated the scene in another picture (picture 5). A black net ensnared two children under the eerie, piercing gaze of the slit-eyed vulture. What sense of dread and despair must have moved the child to paint such a picture?

"How many pictures, did you say, are in this box?" I asked the father. "One thousand five hundred? And only eerie, frightful monsters painted by a child barely six years old!" He nodded with what seemed to be an embarrassed touch of pride.

3

A quote from Max Beckmann came to me: "I painted; that protected me from death and danger."

That was true for Betty as well. She had to paint, driven by her unconscious, in order to survive, lest she be flooded with these frightening pictures which are the mirror images of her inner fears. I understood that she could not sleep, for the creatures she painted by day haunted her also at night in her dreams.

But how was it possible that Betty's mother had not responded to this frightening creativity, to these signals of distress? The wish to talk about Betty had been initiated solely by the father. It seemed too early to pose such questions, however. I simply asked the parents to tell me once more how Betty's fears manifested themselves in everyday life and what she was afraid of.

The mother began. "Well, Betty is, as so many children are today, afraid of the dark, afraid of being left alone, afraid of evil spirits and ghosts, and even afraid of evil eyes."

"And when did this fear of evil eyes appear for the first time, Mrs. Bonsart?"

"My husband and I wanted to leave on a vacation," the mother continued. "Betty was two and a half years old. We took her to an aunt. I reluctantly left her there, because this aunt was a quick-tempered woman. Betty stayed with her for two weeks. She reacted to the separation immediately with vomiting and diarrhea. When I picked her up, she looked weak and sick. All this time she had been quietly withdrawn within herself in her suffering. And it was around this time, in the second half of her third year, that her fear of evil eyes, as Betty calls them herself, first appeared and which has not left her since."

I pulled out another picture which Betty had explained as "Big ghost bites into child's blood" (picture 6). It showed a demon with piercing eyes and a long, sharp beak stabbing the child so that blood flowed from the wound. What fear speaks to us from this picture!

"Have a look at this girl's head (picture 7)," I said. Again there were those oversized eyes from which yellow rays flowed like poisonous streams of tears. A long, arrow-like line entered the violet cavity of the mouth. The head dominated the entire picture; the body was reduced to a few lines. According to Betty's explanation, "mice are growing" out of the head, and from below spiders are running up into it.

In the next picture which the mother pulled forth, (picture 8) Betty had drawn with astounding skill two children again under a gigantic, overpowering eye, as in pictures 3, 4, and 5. To Betty, they were without any will of their own and hence without any self. She drew them as dolls which, after all, are lifeless and are moved only mechanically. She heightened the effect of their lifelessness even further by calling these figures "Broken dolls."

I then asked the parents whether Betty showed any other unusual behavior aside from her fears, sleeplessness, tantrums, and hate for her little brother. The parents pointed out difficulties in

5

eating, saying that Betty often showed strong feelings of nausea toward food, that she suffered from constipation since babyhood, and that she had sucked her thumb for a long time.

"And when did she stop doing that?" "Around the age of four." Mrs. Bonsart said, "I remember, that after returning from a trip I was surprised to find that Betty had given up sucking her thumb. The maid broke her of that habit."

"Broke her of it? You mean by forbidding her to?" I asked. "Thumb-sucking is a comfort to a child, a substitute for something missing; maybe the absent mother?"

"Yes, that may be," Mrs. Bonsart answered, and with a deep sigh she added, "But the children have never been left alone, our maid was always there with them."

"Always the same one?"

"We naturally had to change at times; unfortunately they were not always good, either. When Betty was three, for instance, we had a seventeen-year-old girl. She came from a bad home, her father was an alcoholic. She stayed for two years. Betty once said about her, 'She needs to be spanked and burned.' "

"And how many maids have you had since?"

"Four altogether. But I, too, spend much time at home. True, I have my law office, but I do work at home, so that the children know that I am nearby."

"But with your work, with having to ponder over the letters of the law, is not every distraction and interruption very disturbing to you?"

"That's just it!" Mrs. Bonsart exclaimed. "Indeed, I often feel completely torn. Then I simply have to take off, alone or together with my husband."

"Yes, I can understand that," I said, "then you come back more rested and relaxed. But in the meantime the children are alone with the maid."

"But must you be right there for your children your entire life from morning till evening?" the father put in.

I deliberately left the question unanswered, before countering, "How much time, how many hours have you had for Betty this week?"

Mr. Bonsart leaned back, he seemed to be reflecting in order to face this question honestly, and then replied, "To be honest, not one. I hardly saw her."

No one spoke. There was a long silence. It was as if already in this short time a deeper awareness was making itself felt. This is always painful, always tormenting, because feelings of guilt are aroused.

Then the mother gave a full account of the time during her pregnancy, of the child's birth and earliest infancy. There had been no indications of brain damage to the child at this stage. The parents also could remember no signs of possible congenital mental illness in either of their families, as far as two generations back. Except for constipation since her earliest days, Betty had supposedly had no children's diseases.

Time seemed to fly by in this first talk with

the parents. I looked at my watch and was glad to have scheduled a double session. I wanted to hear more about Betty, about her earliest phase as a baby, and especially about the first mother-child relationship. This first contact decides whether or not a newborn child, who is at first still alienated by its new condition, will gradually come to a positive acceptance of life through a loving, giving mother. For this is the child's only basis of reassurance, the foundation upon which the child must build its confidence in its surroundings and in itself, so that the desire to grow, the wish to live can prevail over the child's wanting to return to its original condition in the womb. In Betty, this tendency probably still was very strong; otherwise she would hardly have painted, or rather, have had to paint so many pictures of embryos.

Together we looked at one of these more closely (picture 9): it was an embryo skillfully sketched in black, encircled by a mass of red, and still attached to a long umbilical cord. The long umbilical cord could be seen again and again in Betty's other embryo pictures. Emotionally, Betty had not yet freed herself from it. She had not yet found that liberating step into life, without which the will to live cannot overcome the wish for death.

How could this have happened?

"While I was still in childbed," Betty's mother reported, "I was told of the death of my step-mother—who had meant very much to me. Upon receiving this news, I collapsed physically and emotionally, and suffered from depression. I could not find any real joy in the baby. I simply had no strength, and could not breast-feed her.

"The demands made on me during the first two years were excessive, especially since I also had to take care of my father's household. Not until Betty was nine months old did I get help. Betty certainly received too little love from me in the first year; on the other hand, I often went to the baby, because she was a comfort to me."

"Thus the child gave more to you than you to her?" The mother remained silent.

We then came to the question of toilet-training. "Well, I started very early with that," the mother reported with a certain pride. "I put Betty on the potty when she was seven months old. It seemed to be a pleasant relief to her, after having suffered from constipation from the start. Therefore she was clean very early—I believe, by the time she was a year and a half. However, I did have to spank her frequently much later, because she started filling doll cups with her urine and then pouring it over the rug."

"And was Betty ever particularly stubborn?" I asked. The mother's immediate answer was: "Betty is always stubborn. She and I live in a continual fight with one another, mostly over clothes."

"And what are these fights like? Can you give me an example?"

"It is always the same story. Betty was three years old—I can still see it as if it were yesterday—we were vacationing on Mallorca and wanted

9

to take a ride on a little boat. Betty was to wear a sailor dress, but she preferred some old pants. During the entire trip she screamed, clinging to her father's pants. We simply could not calm her down. You would have thought she wasn't normal anymore."

"Tell me, what did Betty wear on that trip, the sailor dress or the pants?"

"The sailor dress, of course!" Mrs. Bonsart exclaimed. "Betty still showed this strong resistance when she was four and a half. At this age, all she wanted to be was an Indian girl, wear Indian dresses, braid her hair and decorate herself like an Indian girl. She rebelled every time when I wanted her to wear some other pretty dress instead. But that is how it goes to this day. We lived and live in a continual battle over clothes."

While the mother was talking, I leafed a bit through the drawings and pulled out a series of pictures which offered a deeper insight into this problem. Without comment I handed these pictures to the parents, waiting to see whether or not and to what extent they understood Betty's deeply moving picture language. Silently the three of us looked at these pictures. Then Mrs. Bonsart said, "Where did she see all that?" When the father repeatedly expressed his admiration for Betty's drawing talent, the mother commented, "Yes, Betty has a vivid imagination."

"But maybe Betty wants to express her inner anxiety through these pictures?" I suggested.

The father held up Betty's drawing of the crucified Indian girl. His expression changed; he looked worried. "Then, this Indian girl nailed to the cross is a self-portrait? Is that what you mean?"

"It fits your description of Betty. As you said yourself, she beats her head on the floor and tears out her hair, as if she wanted to destroy herself."

We now looked at a whole series of pictures all of which testified to the same moving outcry as that of the martyred Indian girl. There were trees pierced by arrows and enormous sea-monsters, sharks, and crocodiles, moving with gaping jaws from right to left. There was an Indian girl with long braids hanging nailed to the cross (picture 10). Another picture with the same theme showed Betty as an Indian girl on a blazing pyre with her hands chopped off.

The parents now looked at the pictures with new interest, and also with alarm. "It is indeed remarkable," Mr. Bonsart observed, "that all these threatening animals move from right to left. Is there any unconscious message in this?"

"In the language of symbolism[1] 'right' implies the conscious world, whereas 'left'[2] signifies the unconscious, the self," I explained. "The attack from right to left can be interpreted as a sign of self-destruction, as an aggression directed inward toward the self. As soon as Betty's aggression can be

---

[1] See, for instance, Jolande Jacobi, *Vom Bilderreich der Seele.* (Walter Verlag, Olten).

[2] It is interesting to note in this context that the Latin word 'sinister' means both left and ominous.

redirected through therapy, giving her an outlet, Betty will probably draw all these threatening animals facing from left to right. She might, however, stop painting altogether, or at least paint less, since once she has freed herself of her inner problems such symbolic expression will no longer be of a compelling necessity to her."

My last words seemed to worry the father. "Stop painting altogether," he said slowly. "That would be a shame. Won't psychotherapy have a negative effect on her personality after all? Did not all great works of art arise precisely out of such psychic pressures?"

Now the mother interrupted him. "But after all it is much more important for Betty to become a happy child. When I think back on my childhood, such therapy would have helped me greatly, too." Then she spontaneously began to talk about her childhood. To an adult such experiences may seem trivial, but they can hurt and make a child so insecure that the consequences for life can hardly be overestimated.

Her father was a noted orchestra conductor. Her relationship to him, however, had always been rather cool. When she was sixteen years old, her mother died. Mrs. Bonsart then told of her restless childhood. "I never had a chance to take root anywhere; every year we moved, every year the struggle with unfamiliar cities, new schools, and a strange environment began for me anew. As a child I was exceptionally small—tiny as a matter of fact. I never forget the terrifying experience of having the teacher lift me up by one hand like a doll and exhibit me to the class as the smallest, with the rest of the girls all bursting with laughter. I loathed their laughter and their behavior and affectations in general. Those girls simply had a good cry when something bothered them. I always had to struggle and could not be like they were. I hated those girls. Therefore it was difficult for me to accept the role of a girl. I know I rebelled against it until the age of nine."

Only until the age of nine? I asked myself. Had she not said herself just a few minutes ago, "We still live in a continual fight with one another." Was the unconscious motivation of this struggle with her daughter not the same as in her childhood? Did she not say: "I always had to struggle and could not be like they were. I hated those girls." Here an unresolved problem on her part came to the surface, which unconsciously still determined her attitude toward Betty.

The mother grew more and more animated, telling of her childhood experiences. I clearly felt how these reminiscences brought up old feelings in her. I now understood why—already early in life—she had learned to use her intelligence as a bulwark against painful feelings which otherwise could not have been kept at bay.

While she was talking, her husband watched her with affectionate interest. Maybe it was her outward appearance, too, that pleased him. Her delicate stature and the gentle cut of her pantsuit gave her the air of a medieval page. She was now of normal, average height. Her thick, brown hair was cut in bangs. Warm, brown eyes animated her fine features. To judge by their outward appearance the couple seemed well matched. Mr. Bonsart, too, was slim and wiry, with an inquisitive countenance radiating a good sense of humor, at times playfully mischievous. Compared to his wife, he seemed very lively and more guided by emotion.

Conditions for the therapy of a child are not often as favorable as they were in this case in which both parents showed up together of their own accord and laid down their "chips" without reserve, and—in keeping with all fairness—alternately passed each other the "buck" in attitudes of humorous self-criticism.

Their frankness certainly was encouraged by the atmosphere in which a therapeutic discussion generally is conducted, where everyone feels that he can be an individual with all his faults, where the question is not one of guilt or innocence, and where his feelings and actions are not measured in terms of morality. In such an atmosphere a person can more readily reevaluate and objectify his mistakes and prejudices. In this way an inner transformation can gradually take place; little by little, genuine feelings and intuitive forces move the whole individual to overcome the exclusive control by his intellect and free him from the vicious circle of self-justification.

The scheduled two hours for this first discussion with the parents were drawing to a close. But then Mr. Bonsart began to talk briefly about himself.

"Don't you think Betty will outgrow many of her problems? I mean that as a child I, too, had emotional problems. In Betty I often see myself, all the fears I experienced, and even the notion I had at times of being insane. For a long time I imagined that I was the child of criminals," he continued, "it was an agonizing thought, all the more so since I did not dare talk to anyone about this, because that would only have made matters much worse." Mr. Bonsart told us of his hot-tempered father whose eyes nearly popped out of his head whenever he scolded. "Who knows," he asked, raising his hands, "maybe my exaggerated pleasure in car-racing is also connected to these childhood fears."

"And the way you behave every time another driver gets in your way," his wife put in, "I find such behavior cowardly, because outside of your car you certainly would not rave like that."

In a mixture of humor, earnestness, and self-defense, the father gave us to understand that he undoubtedly got on his family's nerves with certain of his behaviors, especially with his compulsive tidiness, which at times was annoying even to him. "But I can't help it," he added taking a deep breath, "I try to make the best of it."

The conversation turned briefly to Betty. She had entered kindergarten at the age of four. "There Betty had some difficulty in making friends," the mother stated, "but she quickly learned how to cope with that. Using her vivid imagination and other little tricks, she put herself in a leadership position. I didn't like to see her get away with this, fearing that this might make it more difficult for her to outgrow her unpleasant ways."

"Thus you would have preferred," I suggested, "for Betty to have played a secondary or even an inferior role instead of being the leader? But then the same situation as on Mallorca would have arisen, where Betty had to wear the sailor dress instead of her favorite pants?"

Mrs. Bonsart said nothing in response to this. The father, however, quickly saw the connection. Like a little boy, glad to see someone else caught in the act, he rubbed his hands in triumph and said in a frank but warm tone, "My little woman, in this respect you must change. The awful power struggle between you and Betty must end if you want to help her."

"I am trying." She raised her arms and right away let them drop again. "But that is terribly difficult; how can one change oneself?"

We fixed the days for Betty's therapy. Although the parents lived twenty miles outside of Hamburg, they were willing to bring Betty in twice a week. I subsequently learned that the parents lived on the seventh floor of a highrise building where businessmen and women had their offices, fashion and photography studios. There were no playgrounds, and the street, too, was unsuitable for play. Until she entered kindergarten at the age of four, Betty had spent her time in "isolation" with painting. Betty had already passed the entrance examination for the elementary school. She

16

was to start school in four weeks. We then discussed the value of a neurological examination to which the parents gave their consent.

As they prepared to leave, Mr. Bonsart glanced at the box of pictures and said, "If you like, you may keep them here. After everything we learned today from the few pictures we looked at, they undoubtedly will help you come to a deeper understanding of Betty's problems."

"But what good will that do?" Mrs. Bonsart asked. "What's the use of analyzing these pictures? I am interested in hearing from you, Mrs. Ude, how you intend to make Betty well again. What happens in therapy like this?"

I suggested I show them the therapy room where they might more readily picture some of what goes on in child therapy. The parents looked around with interest. While the father headed straight for the swing, the mother examined everything more closely: "What a wonderful, spacious playroom. . . with a large blackboard. . . a puppet theater . . . a real stove to cook on . . . so many party games . . . and a big sandbox . . . guns and boxing gloves with a punching bag! . . . And here a large doll house!" Mrs. Bonsart looked at me inquisitively: "The children, then, play here?"

I did not answer her question immediately. She looked around some more. Then she started to laugh, "What have you got here, even a potty? Is there no toilet down here?"

"Yes, there is," I replied, "but when a child feels like sitting on the potty, he can do so."

17

"But not a child of Betty's age? You are thinking of very small children?"

"Not necessarily."

"Oh, and what have you here? A baby-bottle? Are the children supposed to drink out of it?"

"They aren't *expected* to do anything. Everything you see in this room is simply an invitation. If a child wants to, he can play with these things, but he is not forced or influenced in any way."

"I see. And what do you do if a child does absolutely nothing?" the mother asked, "if nothing happens at all?"

"Something is always happening, even if nothing happens outwardly."

Mrs. Bonsart looked at me in disbelief. "You must have endless patience!"

"It has nothing to do with mere patience. Patience alone will not win you the necessary confidence of a child; and without confidence therapy is not possible."

"To win Betty's confidence will be difficult in any case," Mrs. Bonsart said, "but provided you succeed, what happens next?"

"Then the child will revert, or as the psychologists say, regress to earlier stages of his or her development where it suffered disruptions and unfilled needs. Like a sleep-walker he will set out on his journey to the roots of his troubles to resume— maybe by drinking from the baby-bottle or in using the potty or in spontaneous play; the possibilities are endless—those phases of its life which he did not fully live and outgrow. In reexperiencing the pleasurable and painful feelings associated with these phases, the child can then free himself of his bondage to these disrupted stages of his development."

"All that is very difficult to understand," Mrs. Bonsart said, sighing.

"Maybe the following picture will help you understand better. Imagine yourself swimming across a stream and getting entangled in a liana growing low in the riverbed. You find it difficult to go on swimming or even to keep above water. You must dive down to free yourself from the plants growing below, so that all your strength can be reapplied to the task of crossing the river. The entanglement would correspond to the fixation at an earlier stage of development, for instance, at the oral (concerning the mouth; earliest infancy) phase. To free yourself from that entanglement, you must "regress"—go back to that earlier stage of development—and resolve the problems which are hindering your progress before you can go on with normal development."

"And the child knows how to find its way?" the mother asked skeptically.

"The path is marked out in the child's subconscious. In everything the child does and plays here, the child follows this path in the subjective feeling of freedom; yet, like your dreams which also do not follow any commands, all the child's actions obey an inner urge."

Mr. Bonsart had left the swing and obviously wanted to leave. In parting he mentioned that Betty was inordinately fascinated by flabby rubber toy animals, such as spiders, which she loved to mutilate by tearing out their legs. "A strange behavior," he added thoughtfully. The parents took their leave.

Excerpt from the Neurological Examination

The behavior of the child during the examination was appropriate to the situation. The child was cooperative and made a free and easy impression. Her intelligence was on the level of children her age.

Summary:

The report of the physical examination was normal. No neurological defects were found. Statements by the mother indicated a tendency in the child to neurotic behavior of predominately phobic (excessively fearful) and anankastic nature (pathologically compulsive indicating a pathological compulsion to carry out certain actions already recognized as nonsensical, and inability to suppress certain visions and preconceived notions).

2

"One must always be good . . ."

In order to free Betty of the feeling that she
was coming to me only at her parents' command,
I called her on the telephone and invited her to
our first play session. With this call I also wanted
to help her overcome some of the first feelings
of strangeness between us. When I addressed her,
at first she did not respond at all, but after a pause
she whispered into the telephone, "Yes, my mother
told me about it." The first contact with Betty was
made, weak as it was.

The following day the mother brought Betty for
her first observation session. Betty was a well-built,
pretty girl of normal height, with straight, brown
hair, and a pale complexion. She looked at me
timidly, with a sidewise glance, her eyes cast down.
It was hard for her to part from her mother.
"Mommy, Mommy," she whined when her mother
said goodbye. "When are you coming back? Where
you going? Will you pick me up again?"

At last the mother was able to leave. The two
of us stood alone in the playroom, Betty next to

me with her head bent and her shoulders drooping. Silence filled the room.

Finally Betty climbed onto the rocking-horse. After rocking herself for a while, she asked quietly without looking up, "When is my Mommy coming back?" I pointed to the large clock. "When the arm is there, your Mommy will be back."

I gave her time to soothe herself with rocking. Still, a certain tension remained. With one ear she seemed to be continuously listening to noises coming from the street. Then she anxiously asked me to close the window, so that no one could look in. While gently moving to and fro, she studied the objects in the room. I sat down facing her in the swing, and our mutual soft swinging helped to bridge the strangeness of our first encounter.

We remained this way in silence for a long time. She watched me; then her eyes wandered further around the room, until they stopped at a shelf with a baby-bottle on it. "Can you put milk in it?"

I nodded and pointed to a package with powdered milk. "You can make milk for yourself with that."

She sighed and begged me timidly, "Do it for me, please."

I filled the bottle for her.

"Put this on it, too!" she said helplessly, pointing to the nipple. Contentedly she now sucked the milk, rocking slowly back and forth on the horse. "You have it good. You can make such good milk for yourself!"

Studying me, she said, "You know, you don't seem that strange to me anymore."

To give her some kind of response, I replied, "Well, and we already spoke on the phone with each other."

Suddenly fear stood on her face. "Who just walked past the door?" And shortly afterward, "Was that a bad man?" A little later she asked, "What does he want?" Each time I opened the door, proving to her that there was no one outside. She quieted down a little.

After a few more minutes of rocking, she pointed to the punching-bag. "What's that?"

"That's a bag for boxing," I answered, adding, "If one wants to, one can put on these thick leather gloves and box against it."

This threw her completely off balance. She cried plaintively, "No, no! you have to be good always!" She was waiting for me to confirm this.

I shrugged my shoulders. "If one can."

Now she was even more upset and insisted, "One must always, *always* be good!"

"Well," I said, "there is day and night, light and darkness, and there is also good and bad."

My answer obviously made her uncomfortable. She left the rocking-horse in order to turn away from me and went to the puppet theater where she picked up the crocodile and cautiously made it open its jaw. I put my hand in it.

"Don't be afraid," she said, "it doesn't bite, it's tame."

"A tame crocodile?" and I looked at her doubtingly.

"All animals are tame, even this wolf here,"

24

Betty returned, pointing to a little wolf amidst many objects, animals, and human dolls in the opened Sceno-box. With the help of the Sceno-box the so-called Sceno-test is performed. It offers concrete and immediate insight into a person's emotional attitude toward those people and objects in the world, which immediately affect his psychological make-up. The effective attraction of this play-test lies in its soliciting character; in this miniature world the person can cope with his personal and material surroundings in form of pliable dolls and many other materials.

"If you like, you could build something with these things."

Betty instantly got to work. First she placed a little Christmas tree in the middle of the building board. Under the tree she put a baby. Then she let a fox and a gander circle round the baby and said with a sustained hissing sound, "Here comes the bad fox sneaking up." (Here gander and fox are symbolic representations for her feelings of hate and jealousy toward her little brother).

Next she busied herself for some time with the little toilet, and was pleased to find a toilet brush to go with it. She rummaged further in the Sceno-box and picked out the crocodile, reporting that she had a flabby spider and many other flabby animals at home. "Oh, I like them so much! I tore out their legs, just tore them out, because they made me mad!" Again her voice had a hissing quality.

She reached for the large cow, struggled with

it briefly, and placed it in the far corner of the building board. Directly in front of the cow she put the crocodile which she had put aside before, and said, "Huuugh, this is getting dangerous now." (In this "Sceno" Betty confirmed her own aggressive tendencies toward her mother. The cow is a mother figure; the crocodile a symbol of aggression. Her multilation of the toy spiders, a female symbol, also reveals these tendencies). With this she let me know that she had finished with her set-up.

To my question, "And where are you in this game?" she answered, "I'm not there!" She sat down on the rocking-horse again. This rocking back and forth seemed to do her good.

In order to get more test questions answered, I was more active in this first session than I would be on later occasions. I now picked up the Kasper-puppet[1] and let Kasper address Betty.

"A child wakes up, screams, and says, 'I had a bad dream.' What could it have dreamed?"

Betty immediately took this question personally, and answered excitedly, "I always have very, very bad dreams—about ghosts and wicked spirits—" She began to stammer. "I was with my Mommy. We stood in front of something dark—under a bridge—there was a black man, and I was so afraid. He had very evil eyes—" She moaned, "I'm always so afraid of evil eyes. In my dreams I'm always

---

[1] Translator's note: Kasper: a good-hearted, jolly-faced puppet who figures in every German puppet show as an announcer, confidant of the audience, a helper in need, etc.

afraid." Telling this dream affected her strongly. She rocked more vigorously, and I gave her some time before the next question.

Kasper asked once more, "A child says, I'm so afraid. What could it be afraid of?" Again she took the question personally, "I'm afraid of open doors, of bad men, that burglars might come in and do something bad to me."

Suddenly, with a suspicious and searching glance, she looked me directly in the eye. "What if you're not Mrs. Ude at all? What if you're an evil man who changed himself into Mrs. Ude?" A nervous twitching became visible on her fine little face. I noticed that her left eyelid drooped slightly. She looked exhausted.

"You mean transformed by magic like in a fairy-tale?" I asked.

"Yes, that's what I mean."

"That you must find out for yourself, just like in the fairy-tales. In them there are good and wicked fairies. The wicked fairies cast a spell on you, and the good fairies help free you from that spell."

She continued to rock restlessly to and fro. Although the milk bottle was empty by now, she frequently put the nipple in her mouth. She watched me and finally said, "I believe you are a good fairy. But sometimes it's the witches in fairy-tales, who cast spells on you."

"Yes, that's right," I replied, "and then one must be very brave and walk through a large forest and overcome many dangers before one can get free of the spell."

She breathed deeply, "That must be hard—" Unexpectedly she then asked, "May I now come more often to see you?"

"Yes, Betty, if you like."

"And what will we do here?"

"Whatever you like to do. You, Betty, say what you want us to play. We can cook, dig in the sand, knead, paint, play with the puppets, and do many other things—whatever pleases you."

"And then only I'll come, and no other children?"

"These hours belong to you alone."

She got off her rocking-horse, clapped her hands and exclaimed, "That'll be wonderful! Only I will come to you, just me, and no other children." She ran to the table where a jar stood filled with candy. "May I take some?" she asked timidly.

"Yes, you may."

Hesitantly she took out one candy, then two, and remarked, "I need candy soooo badly, but my Mommy won't buy any for me. She says sweets are not good for my teeth. But I need them so much. Can you make candies rain from the sky?"

"Like in never-never land," I smiled, "where you can eat your way through a mountain of sweets?"

Instantly her imagination took off with her; she listed all the wonderful things one could gobble up in never-never land: gigantic heaps of chocolate, candy, marzipan. She sighed, "It must be beautiful in never-never land."

I pointed to the arm of the big clock. "Look, Betty, in a few minutes your hour is over."

"And when do I come again?"

"You will come twice a week, every Tuesday and Friday."

"That's tomorrow already?"

"No, tomorrow is Saturday and then comes Sunday—"

"And then I'll come again," she interrupted me.

"No, Betty, first comes Monday and then Tuesday, and that is the day you come again."

She begged, "But why can't I come tomorrow?"

"Only twice a week, Betty, and that is every Tuesday and Friday."

"And only the two of us will play together? No other children?"

"Only the two of us all by ourselves, Betty! But now you must go."

Betty's mother was already waiting outside. I left them alone, but still heard the mother asking in dismay, "Why are you tearing out your hair, Betty?" (A child who has only a numbed awareness of its own self, of its own body, and who has the feeling of not really being there at all, sometimes develops the symptom of tearing out its own hair as a means of restoring through pain the lost contact with its body and with its very existence. On the other hand, to inflict pain on one's self is a way of coping with unconscious aggressive impulses, by directing them toward one's self.)

I recalled her father's last remark. "Betty is inordinately fascinated by spiders which she loves to mutilate by tearing out their legs. A rather strange behavior," he had added thoughtfully. And Betty, too, had talked about a flabby spider whose

29

legs she tore out because it annoyed her. I brought out the box with Betty's pictures and found many drawings of such spidery animals with long tentacles. Of one of these Betty had said, according to her father's footnote, "That is an animal which fells trees;" of another, "That is a terrible animal with a chopped-off tree root." (Over the ages, the tree has been the symbol of man and man's individuation. A common example is the image of the tree of life).

The next picture (picture 11) impressed me especially. Betty had called it a "Portrait of a Woman."

Notice that she drew the woman without arms and entirely in black (the color of depression and grief). The two enormous tentacles, which she placed around the portrait, dominate nearly the entire picture and leave no room for movement for the laced up, armless figure pressed into the right corner. This figure, as well as the chopped-off tree, undoubtedly represented Betty's self.

What the mother had said in our first conversation, was definitely true also for Betty's attitude toward her mother: "We live and lived in a continual fight with one another."

Betty's delight in tearing out the spiders' legs was an unconscious expression of her struggle against the negative aspect of her mother image. It became obvious to me that without intimately involving Betty's mother in this therapy that I would hardly be able to help Betty.

3

"There are rats . . . they grub and gnaw, sometimes they are in the attic too, or in the cellar."

Tuesday had arrived and with it Betty's second hour of therapy. Without saying a word, she headed straight for the swing to cradle herself. She remained silent.

I sat down facing her on a bench that was slightly removed. I felt clearly that it was still necessary to keep a physical distance between us. Quietly withdrawn, she swung to and fro, her head drooping a little. Her face revealed an inner strife.

It was important that I not interrupt such phases of silence with insignificant questions. Doing that would only be disturbing the course on which her unconscious was leading her.

Finally, she began, "We were late—we are always late; and I wanted so much to be early at Mrs. Ude's." Her voice had a stubborn tone.

I looked at the clock: "You are exactly on time, Betty."

She was swinging restlessly. "Lisa combed me nicely. My mother said you would not like me if I wasn't combed nicely." She looked up.

"I always like you, Betty, just as you are, whether

you are well combed or not; whether you are sad or happy."

"You'll always like me—even if I do something bad some time?"

"Even then. One cannot always be good."

There was another pause.

"I wonder what the other children in the city will say?" she asked.

Although I knew very well that her jealousy and fear of being abandoned had prompted this question, I asked, "What do you mean by that, Betty?"

"There are so many children in the city. What if they all come to you?" I hesitated with my answer; and right away she burst forth, "I don't want other children to come! Would other children come when I am here?"

"When you have your hour no other child will come, Betty!"

"I'm here all by myself?"

"You don't have to share your hour with anyone."

"And you wouldn't let anybody in either?"

"I would let no one in, Betty."

"Could you lock the door?"

"If you like, I can do that too."

"That's good, then we're here all by ourselves." She jumped from the swing and discovered the string of candy hanging from the ceiling. "It's raining candy from the sky, just like I wished!" Frantically she tore them all from the ceiling, raking them blissfully into a heap. "And now we'll eat sweets, many sweets. And we'll bake a cake."

She ran to the stove. "I'd like to cook some porridge . . . but I won't eat it. Food makes me sick. I just like to slop around and make a real hodgepodge." She went to the sandbox, cautiously dribbled water over the sand, and let it trickle through her fingers. Some of it spilled on the floor. She was startled. "Does it matter if I get things dirty here sometimes?"

"No, Betty, not at all."

Next she picked up some clay. I joined her, and we both worked the clay, squeezing "mud sausages," as she called them, from our hands. She visibly enjoyed this.

Then she formed a rat and placed it on the rim of the sandbox. Suddenly she looked in dismay at her soiled hands. She was seized by disgust, seemed to feel miserable, and dashed to the sink where she tried to regain her composure by a long and involved cleaning process. She now stood before me with wet hands. A new problem arose: "What shall I dry my hands on?" she whined. The stack of clean towels filled her with loathing. She smelled every one, rejecting each in disgust. She was in despair. Finally she brought herself to dry her hands with Kleenex tissues.

She sat down in the swing again. This gentle movement always seemed to do her good. She was silent. Footsteps outside the window alarmed her. I had to check the doors and windows to make certain that they were really locked.

After a while she started to talk again, "There are rats. They live under ground. They grub and gnaw. Sometimes they're in the attic too, or in the cellar."

"Yes, Betty, such things exist."

She continued, "It is bad when there're rats in the house."

"It must be bad, Betty, when there're rats in the house." I clearly felt how this dialogue, conducted entirely on the level of the unconscious, did her good. She had to hear from me the unmitigated admission that I too knew how bad it is when rats are in the house. (Rats were the destructive, aggressive power in the house—her own self.)

Rats must have occupied Betty greatly. The first animal she had formed with the clay at the beginning of this hour was a rat. I remembered a drawing by her, in which a gigantic rat was running inside of a head from right to left. "Rat in the mind" Betty had called this picture (picture 12). (See also picture 7, where mice are growing out of a girl's head.)

It is indeed bad "when there are rats in the house," when a person's aggressions are pent up inside him, ravaging him, as demonstrated by Betty's self-destructive beating of her head and tearing out her hair. But if he lets them out, they will attack the people around him, whom he doesn't want to hurt, fearing they will no longer love him. An insecure child like Betty had special reason to be afraid of not being loved since the lack of attention in her infancy had left her without a basis of confidence in unconditional love.

Absorbed in these thoughts, I heard Betty say,

"I feel so hot." She wiped her hand over her forehead. "I always sweat so easily!" In the next moment she started to take off her dress and her socks.

Fear makes one sweat; in this case even the tranquilizers that had been prescribed earlier for Betty were of no avail.

She sat down in the sandbox again and mumbled to herself, listlessly letting sand trickle through her fingers. Then she dug a deep hole in the sand: "There are bogs, people sink away in them, and then the corpses stay way down there forever."

"Yes," I returned, "there are bogs, but there are firm paths which lead across the bogs and when one follows these, one doesn't sink away." She looked at me. Fear was on her face. "Where did you see a bog?" I asked, and Betty told me of a visit to a museum with her mother, where she had seen such a bog. It was typical for this fear-ridden child that of the many displays in the museum only this all-engulfing bog should have stuck in her mind. In a picture she had expressed this fear of being swallowed (picture 14).

On the left hand side, the side of the unconscious, a frightening head with a gaping mouth is being attacked by a crocodile. The head is reminiscent of one of the three Gorgonian sisters in Greek mythology,[1] of the hideous woman's face whose

[1] Mythical figures are archetypes of the collective unconscious; that is, in creating myths, mankind unconsciously projects essential, ever-valid truths.

glance turns the beholder to stone. By means of a long cord, which can be regarded as an umbilical cord, two children are entangled in this dramatic scene. In the upper right corner Death appears again.

The psychic drama represented in this picture cannot be merely interpreted as the struggle between the personal mother and the child. Rather, this picture expresses an absolute fear of death, of being swallowed up, of sinking away into the eternal abyss, for which the wolf disguised as the grandmother in "Little Red Riding Hood" is a fitting image in the child's world of imagination. Betty's second play session was coming to an end. "Look at the clock, Betty; we have only two minutes left."

Somewhat distractedly she got up, put on her dress and socks, and went over to the snack table. She held the long string of candy in her hands. A fleeting smile brightened her face. "May I take them with me?"

"They were meant for you, Betty!"

As she walked out, she said, "Now I shall live from one piece of candy to the next, until I come back."

"And that is very soon, Betty."

4

"I don't even want to sleep anymore."

On Thursday my phone rang early in the morning. "Hello, Mrs. Ude here." No answer. "Hello? Who is calling?"

Then I heard an outcry, the heartbreaking weeping of a child. It was Betty. She could hardly speak. She stammered in despair, "It is so bad, so so bad, Mrs. Ude! I always have such awful dreams—about ghosts and very wicked spirits!" She wept and wept. Now and then she could bring herself to speak in painful fragments. "It will never get better, I always have such bad dreams; and then I talk about them, but then I have more bad dreams. And I always have to think of them. And it never stops. I don't even want to sleep anymore." She could speak no more; she was sobbing and needed time to recover. Then came her question: "Can you help me, Mrs. Ude?"

"Yes, Betty. The day will come when you will no longer have dreams about wicked spirits. Believe me, Betty, it will get better."

"Can't I come see you today? Please!"

"But you know, Betty, that you have your hour every Tuesday and Friday. You'll come tomorrow, and then we will play together."

I heard a deep sigh. "I'm so jealous, Mrs. Ude. But I do come to see you all alone."

"You have your hour all alone; all to yourself, Betty."

She seemed to have calmed down a little, yet I gave her another reassurance: "You can always call me, if you like, just as you did now."

"Yes," she said, "Lisa has your phone number."

"Did Lisa dial the number for you just now?"

"Yes, she did."

"When you come tomorrow, Betty, then we'll practice how you yourself can dial the number. You'll see it's very easy." She did not answer.

"Shall we do that, Betty?"

"Yes," she said in a low voice.

She did not have the strength to say good-bye and to hang up. So I took over the mutual exchange of good-byes.

Betty herself had found a lifeline which she could use whenever extreme fears threatened to overwhelm her.

In this telephone conversation Betty had for the first time addressed me with the familiar form "Du," instead of her former polite "Sie" which in German is used with adult strangers.

This subtle change was a promising sign of confidence in me.

5

"Push the hair out of your face."

It was Friday, and Betty arrived punctually for her hour. She pressed something into my hands: "I baked these for you." Two death-skulls and a skeleton.

Betty hung herself over the swing, letting her head, arms, and legs dangle. She swung slowly to and fro and suddenly began spitting on the floor. She kept this up for quite some time. Apparently she wanted to rid herself of subconscious feelings of disgust. Sitting upright in the swing, she looked at me and said, "Push the hair out of your face!" Her swinging continued as she made statements such as, "You never wear pants! Next time put on a pair of pants!"

From the manner of her speech, I sensed some problem hidden in her criticism. I made no response.

In a moment she was swinging more restlessly. Then she burst forth, "I don't like pants either!" Her expression grew somber. "But my mother forced me to wear these pants. I think my mother doesn't want you to like me." She fixed her eyes on me, probably waiting for an answer. I remained silent, however. Words and explanations can be encouraging at times, but in this case they only would have constricted her. She had to sense—from the way I looked at her and listened—that I understood her fully. Then she continued, "But you always like me, no matter what I'm wearing."

"Yes, Betty, I like you the way you are."

While swinging on, she said softly as if to herself that she felt so tired. Again, her face twitched nervously. Her left eyelid drooped. She seemed forlorn and distracted. She asked for the baby-bottle. Again I had to fill it with milk and fit the nipple on it. Sucking it with half-closed eyes and rocking back and forth, she whispered, "I'm a baby."

I was still being careful to keep a sufficient physical distance between us. Too much closeness seemed to make her uneasy. Betty remained this way for some time. We did not speak. Outwardly nothing happened, yet much took place in Betty. By letting herself be a baby, she could satisfy needs which had remained unfulfilled from her infancy stage of development, and gradually free herself of her fixation at this stage. The emotional energy thus set free, would assist her in the long process of growth still lying ahead. Betty grew more relaxed. Now and then a contented smile settled briefly on her face. At last she had enough strength to leave the swing. She placed the baby-bottle back on the shelf and with an air of decision said, "Let's play birthday now. Mrs. Ude has a birthday, and I'll come to visit you." Full of enthusiasm she now collected beautiful gifts for me. She wrapped the imaginary presents in colored paper, tied ribbons

40

around them, decorated them with feathers which she tore from an Indian headdress, attached candies to the packages, and then came to congratulate me. Decorating the rocking-horse with colored ribbons to which she also tied candies, she exclaimed happily, "This here is our house. We're all alone here, and Mrs. Ude is always good."

She also brought the wolf and the crocodile to congratulate me. "To these animals too, you must always be good," she said beseechingly.

"Even if they are mean to me?"

"They never are mean; they're always good," she insisted. She laid the wolf and the crocodile on the table. "Don't be afraid, they won't bite you. I'll feed them well, then they won't need to eat people." She fetched the baby-bottle and gave some milk to the wolf.

Wiping her forehead with her hand, she remarked, "I'm sweating—yesterday, too. I took off all my clothes. My mother scolds me when I do that. She says I'll get sick." Instantly she took off her sweater and shoes, and pranced about the room. At the snack table she rejoiced at seeing all the sweets. Yet most of them she did not like. Sniffing at every candy, she expressed her disgust, and then started to sort them: the ones she didn't like, she intended for her brother Sebastian, the few remaining ones she tucked away in her pocket.

Suddenly she became very active. "I still have so much to do today, I must do the wash." She poured large quantities of soap into the basin, collected everything that looked washable, pronounced it to be dirty laundry, and eagerly began to wash.

It struck me that while she was washing, she talked much about Sebastian who was coming with Lisa to pick her up today, and for whom she still had to cook something delicious. Her laundering gradually became painful to her. She complained and moaned that the laundry wasn't getting clean enough and that the stains remained. She could not put an end to it. Her dismay increased when I pointed out that the hour would be over in five minutes. She lamented and begged, "Let me stay longer. Please! I still have to make everything nice for Sebastian." I repeated that she had only five more minutes. With that she left off the laundering and plunged into her preparations for Sebastian. "He shall have delicious, sweet soups to drink." She tore open one package after another, pouring everything into a pot. Then she filled the baby-bottle, set the table and put a pillow on Sebastian's chair and a soft sheep-skin on the floor. "Everything has to be nice for him." (Betty was caught in a vicious circle. With her compulsive, painful laundering and her efforts to spoil Sebastian, she was trying to silence her unconscious feelings of guilt toward her brother. Not until she could overcome her severe existential fears would she stop feeling threatened by her brother, would her hate and feelings of guilt disperse, and a genuine sisterly love develop.) It all happened in a whirl, and the next minute Lisa and Sebastian came to pick up Betty.

42

It seemed advisable to me to say good-bye at this time, lest I get involved in a situation which would force me to take sides. This was because in everyday life the rules which make living together possible must be observed, whereas in therapy they are—at least partially—suspended in order to bring about emotional release for the patient. From a distant corner I watched the final scene through the open door.

Sebastian wanted none of the "sweet soups." Betty was disappointed. But she did not give in and tried to push other sweets on him. All in vain. As a last resort she tried to shove the baby-bottle into his mouth. This undertaking was an utter failure.

When Betty, in frustration, sucked at the bottle herself, Lisa remarked, "Sebastian doesn't take the bottle anymore, he's too big for that."

This hint hit Betty hard. A bad scene followed, with Betty screaming desperately, "I'm no baby! I'm not a baby! Only Sebastian. Always Sebastian!" In vain Lisa tried to comfort her. They left the house with Betty howling.

6

"If a bad man comes and shoots arrows into Cille's tummy, don't scream, otherwise the police will come . . ."

Betty arrived punctually, swinging a little purse. She was pleased that we both were wearing Bavarian Dirndl dresses. Stopping in front of me, she gave me a cursory glance, and said as she had before, "Push the hair out of your face."

She then walked resolutely to the table, emptied her little purse filled with chocolate and candies, and commented, "I brought you these today. My mother said you were poor, and that I mustn't take so much candy from you." She looked at me questioningly "Is that true, are you poor?"

"No, Betty, I'm not poor. Your mother doesn't know that, but now you can tell her."

"May I then go on cooking at your house?"

"Naturally, Betty."

"And also take candy home with me?"

"Yes, you can do that."

She was relieved. "That's good!" she exclaimed. "You know, I need sweets so badly." And in the next instant she was at the stove, greedily tearing open all the packages and rejoicing at the enormous heap of raisins, oat flakes, powdered milk, and raspberry syrup. While she blissfully stirred this around, she remarked, "The heap ought to be much bigger yet." (Betty's pathological desire for sweets, as well as her unrestrained craving for possessions in general, revealed how unsatisfactory her oral phase must have been. Betty still had a strong fixation at this first phase in an infant's development.) For the first time the oat flakes tasted especially good to her. She was stuffing them into her mouth with cupped hands.

She eyed the Sceno-box. She wanted me to give her many things from it: the sparkling red garnet, the animals, the little mugs, etc. She wanted to have everything.

It seemed that Betty would have liked best to plunder the whole playroom. "You can't take any of that with you, Betty. All the toys must stay here." She did not give in; she begged and bargained. I remained firm. In order to give her an outlet for her pent-up, high-flying wishes, I suggested that she dictate to me a list of the things she would like. I said that by the time of our next session I would decide which items I could give to her.

The floodgates opened. She dictated, "A little Christmas tree, a shiny gem, a whistle, an angel, chicks, snowmen, necklaces, rings, little monkeys, and candies—plenty of candy." Her wishes filled an entire page. "Did you get it all down right?" she asked anxiously.

"Yes, Betty!"

"Read it to me once more."

She listened with close attention and obvious satisfaction as if she had already been given everything.

She then put her little hands on the table, one on top of the other, and pressed her forehead on them.

What was going on inside her?

"I must tell you something," she began still in her bent-over position. "Last night I had a very bad dream again. It was a big candle—a gigantic finger touched it, and from this finger another awful finger branched off. I was so scared. It was a very bad dream," she moaned.

Just then, something scratched at the door. It was "Cille," my little dog, a cocker spaniel. Betty loved dogs and begged me to let Cille in. Cille immediately threw herself on her back at my feet and rolled around on the sheep skin, wanting her belly rubbed. Betty watched.

"Is it a boy or a girl?" she asked.

"A girl, Betty. You can tell by her many little teats on her belly."

Betty looked at these for a while in complete silence. Then she grew restless, turned to me anxiously, and said, "If a bad man comes now and shoots arrows into Cille's tummy, you mustn't scream!"

"I shouldn't scream then?"

"No, no, no!" she returned excitedly. "You mustn't scream, otherwise the police will come!"

"You don't want the police to come, Betty?"

"No, no, the police mustn't come; otherwise they'll ask who did it!"

"And we don't want to tell them, Betty?" I asked in a low voice.

"No, no, no!" she cried out and said no more. I did not press her further. It was as if she had lost the thread of her thoughts.

I sat down to draw, busying myself with a sketch-pad and colored pencils. I thought Betty might seize the opportunity to draw and bring out her unconscious problem.

It wasn't long before she, too, sat down at the table. She drew a yellow sun (picture 13).

"It is very hot, and the rays are evil fingers, they all are evil fingers."

"As in your dream, Betty?" She did not answer. I looked at her sun and said casually, "They could also be arrows. The sun is shooting arrows into the earth."

Betty did not respond to this. She was totally unconscious of the problem that brought on her fear. She could give no verbal expression to it, so I did not press her further.

She wandered around the room restlessly seemingly unable to decide what to do. Again she listened to noises from the street. "Who is walking by?" She was afraid that somebody might look in through the windows. With her index finger she lightly touched the baby-bottle. "Lisa said that big girls shouldn't drink from a baby-bottle." Betty had not forgotten the disastrous end of the previous session.

"But here they may, Betty. Here big girls may do anything they feel like doing. If they want to, they may even be babies." She wanted me to fill the bottle and place the nipple on it. Swaying gently back and forth in the swing, she sucked on it in comfort.

When the clock struck announcing the end of her hour, Betty became restless. She did not want to leave yet. Her sucking took on a desperate, biting nature. Questions poured forth: "Why can't I stay longer? Why can't I come every day?" She ran to the snack table to pick up raisins, oatmeal, and candies to take home with her. I offered her a plastic bag to carry them in. She sniffed at it and threw it aside. "It stinks! Don't you have a different one?" Each new, perfectly clean bag evoked the same reaction of disgust. At last she found a solution. She tucked up her dress in order to carry everything off in it. Slightly embarrassed, she looked at me, saying, "I need them so badly. And you really are not poor, Mrs. Ude?!"

"No, I'm not, Betty."

"And don't forget my list of wishes!"

"On Friday there will be something from that list on the table."

"Be sure not to forget."

"Definitely not."

"On Friday I'll come again!"

"Every Tuesday and Friday you come."

"And I can always call you on the phone when I want to?"

"You can always call me, Betty."

Finally she was ready to leave. I stood alone in the room, lost in thought and filled with concern about her. Once more I picked up Betty's drawing of the sun (picture 13).

The sun is a male symbol, a symbol of the procreative force. (The rays of the sun penetrate the earth: the earth is a feminine symbol; one also refers to it as mother earth. It is revealing in this context to remember that in the Romance languages the gender of the word for sun is masculine and that the god representing the sun—Apollo—is masculine in various religions.) Betty had called the rays of this sun—"evil fingers." As I stared at the picture, the resemblance of these fingers to a penis was startling. The problem Betty had expressed in this picture also haunted her dream of the large candle with the awful finger and prompted her remark about Cille: ". . . an evil man comes and shoots arrows into Cille's tummy." In each case it was the same fear of a penis penetrating a female body. This was unusual enough, but why this fear of the police? The police stand for the super-ego or the conscience, for fear of punishment. Fear of punishment arises from feelings of guilt, even if one is not aware of these feelings. The police are also called the eyes of the law. Betty's fear of evil eyes was embedded in the same set of problems as was her fear of the police in her experience with the dog. This same fear can be traced in picture 6, "Big ghost bites into child's blood," and in picture 7, "Girl's head with arrow-like lines penetrating her mouth." Once again I leafed through the notes which I had taken right after each session. The last two times Betty started out with the same remark: "Push the hair out of your face!" What was she trying to say? My hair was already back from my forehead. Strange? Betty's mother wore bangs! Through an unconscious projection Betty was seeing something that did not exist in reality: bangs on my forehead.

It seemed that a fear was mounting in Betty, the fear of transferring upon me her negative feelings toward her mother. Betty was apprehensive of this and therefore she unconsciously imagined something which did not exist.

She was still wooing me, by bringing me flowers and birthday gifts; but she had already made the entreaty to me: "You must always be good," (even to bad animals such as the wolf and crocodile) as if she sensed an outbreak of her aggressions toward me.

7

"I always have to wear what I don't want to . . ."

When Betty stepped in at her next session, the first things that caught her eye were my shoes. "Why are you wearing sandals?" she criticized. "It's raining today; then you wear walking shoes!"

She headed straight for the swing, rocked back and forth, looked down at her pants, and burst forth, "I wanted to wear yellow pants today, but my mother insisted on the red ones!" I clearly felt her mounting anger. Her face reddened. "I always have to wear what I don't want to," she exploded, "And that makes me furious!" She swung excitedly, looking at me with flashing eyes. Since her outrage contained no question, I remained completely passive. Gradually her swinging slowed down a little.

"Did you think of my list of wishes?"

"Go and look at the table, Betty!"

She was at the table in no time and exclaimed, "You bought the little Christmas tree for me, which I wanted so much. I knew it, I knew you wouldn't forget it!" She picked it up, gleefully dancing around in circles. "And what kind of sweets do you have for me? Sugar pops, for the first time, sugar pops!" Right away she ate heartily of them.

"You must always buy a whole lot of them!" While still chewing, she remembered what she wanted to do that day. "Let's cook pudding for Sebastian and my Mommy. They love pudding. Hurry, we must not lose any time." Without delay she turned to the cooking corner where she enthusiastically tore open all the packages and indiscriminately mixed instant pudding, oat flakes, sugar, raspberry syrup, and powdered milk. She stirred the enormous heap in a state of bliss. Meanwhile she commanded, "Now you do only what I tell you to." The orders followed at once. But everything, simply everything, I did was wrong. When I tried to defend myself, she snapped, "Don't interrupt me! Set the table! Take off that smock of yours, I can't stand it." She went on, "No, the armchair goes *there*; no, the candle *there*; no, *there* the bowl, and with this fork only my Mommy and I may eat. You can eat nothing with my fork." When I sat down at the table before she did, she yelled at me, "Get up, you may not sit down until I tell you to!"

When we were seated at the table at last, Betty served my portion to me. As I reached for the bowl of my own accord, she tore it from my hand, flying into a rage. "You can't have more until I tell you!" With this she upset the milk bottle and scolded, "Now I have to get up again and fetch a rag. But this is the last time!" When I accidentally knocked over the candle, making it fall into the pudding bowl, she flared up and, with her eyes flashing, abused me like an old shrew.

52

In my therapy room nearly everything was available. The potty which Betty's mother had commented on stood on the floor below the bookshelf. It was not easily visible, but Betty discovered it. She went straight for it and holding it up, said, "Let's make a room-toilet now for ourselves." Alternately Betty put the wolf and the crocodile on the potty and commanded, "You have to go poopoo now!" Then she pretended to flush, accompanying this with a "swish" sound.

"And now I'll sit on it," Betty announced resolutely. She "built" the toilet in a corner where she could lean comfortably against the wall. Apparently feeling much at ease there, she began to tell me how it always hurt her to have a bowel movement because her feces were always so hard. She talked about toilets which sometimes stank badly, but she thought this one was especially comfortable.

Gradually her rambling took on a distinctly sensual nature. (Because Betty had been toilet-trained overly early, she had not been able to fully live the anal phase which follows the oral phase in an infant's development. Betty was now making up for this in order to free herself from her fixation at this phase. An anal complex is associated with compulsions regarding a person's sense of cleanliness and orderliness. Overzealous toilet-training and exaggerated taboos can lead to an obsession with cleanliness and to pedantry or to their opposites: indifference to filth and chaotic disorder.) "Everybody has to go poopoo," she continued, "me and you, my Mommy and Daddy, all people and all dogs, Cille, too. Mice make little droppings, but for the mice those are just as big as the sausages are for us." She started to use stronger language. Next she used the word "shit." "At Gerdi's, there is shit stuck on the toilet sometimes." She giggled, "When you go poopoo, you need paper, but not when you go peepee, then nothing sticks to your behind. You know," she continued after awhile, "I already went potty when I was still a baby. I was clean very early, my Mommy said, but Sebastian, he doesn't make anything in the potty, he waits until he has his diapers back on and then he makes a mess in them, he likes that better."

Every time she defecated, she looked up at me with round eyes, "That was a big one again, and how it stinks!" Then she demanded paper and cleaned herself off. As I carried out the potty, she put forth self-confidently, "You do that for me gladly, don't you?"

After this she declared herself to be dead tired. Indeed she did look pale and exhausted. She dragged herself to the couch where she huddled in a corner with her legs drawn up and asked for the milk bottle.

She wondered aloud, "What exactly are you? A doctor or a student?" I explained to her that it was my profession to help children by playing with them.

"Then, you are a child play-helper?" Her eye-lids grew heavy. She spoke more and more slowly like a baby shortly before going off to sleep. "You help the children," she added and slipped the nipple back in her mouth; musing, she added sleepily, "Do you also help grown-ups?" As I was trying to think of an appropriate answer, Betty suggested, "They don't need to be helped, they can help themselves."

The clock struck the hour. "Did you hear that, Betty? Our time is up." Reluctantly she arose, slipped into her coat, pocketed a handful of candy, and left the room.

8

"Mrs. Ude tastes of blood."

I greeted Betty at the front door. She immediately commanded me, "Put on a pair of pants right now; it's cold, then you have to wear pants."

I shrugged my shoulders casually. "But I'm not cold, I'd rather be wearing this dress."

"Don't talk back to me," she snapped, "it's cold and you have to wear pants, period." With that she stamped her foot on the floor.

"Ah," I said, feigning sullenness, "maybe next time, if it's cold. It would take too long to change now. After all we want to play."

"Well, okay then," she grumbled and walked ahead of me into the playroom. She sat down on a little stool and unwrapped a package from which she produced a pair of sandals. "These are my favorite shoes," she explained, "but my mother can't stand them. She always hides them from me so that I can't find them. It makes me mad."

"I can certainly understand that," I said.

This day, again, Betty felt too hot, and boldly undressed down to her undershirt and panties. She squatted down at the table, and propping her elbows on it, she leaned her head on her opened hands.

She pushed candies into her mouth, stating that that day she needed sweets more than ever.

After awhile she fetched the big cow from the Sceno-box, placed it before her and put a piece of fur around its neck. I thought that perhaps her need for more motherly tenderness prompted this gesture. Then she took out a male figure, and declared, "That is Daddy." And a joyful smile brightened her face.

Again she went to the swing where she gently rocked herself back and forth for some time. I watched her in silence and was struck by the repeated sudden rolling of her eyes. The nervous twitching in her face also seemed to me to occur more frequently than it had. Several minutes passed this way. I waited patiently at a distance and left the direction of the hour to her. Suddenly she announced, "Today we'll bake a gigantic cake for Mommy and Sebastian." She started giving orders. "Turn on the stove. Sit down on the couch and don't budge." Meanwhile she heaped ingredients into the mixing bowl. In between she let waterdrops fall onto the hot heating plate, taking delight in the resulting hissing and steam. She continued to boss me around. "Lie down on the couch! My Mommy sometimes does that, too."

Then with a witch-like snickering, Betty suddenly began throwing building blocks, balls and similar little items at me. I had to protect myself with a thick pillow. In a flash she increased her attack and hurled a shower of every small object she could lay her hands on at my head. In the next moment

57

she stood over me, snatched the pillow from my head, crushed it back onto my head, and threw her full weight down on me.

It was clear. She wanted to destroy me. Her contorted face betrayed shocking hatred and endless despair. She uttered a piercing cry: "Now you're acting like a crocodile, like a pig!" and screamed over and over again, "Stop that stupid laughing!"

She spat in my face.

Then she fled to the swing and cried out, "Mrs. Ude tastes of blood."

Suddenly everything passed as if a spell had been lifted. Betty gave the impression of having no memory of the incident, as if the memory of it were completely lost. She also did not feel hot anymore. Of her own accord she put on her skirt and sweater. Again she took refuge in the state of earliest infancy. She demanded the baby-bottle and curled up with it in a soft armchair.

"Push me," she begged, and I now pushed her around the room in the armchair as if it were a baby carriage. We still had much time. While I was rolling her about, she once said softly, "Frau Udelein." She closed her eyes and relaxed completely. In this way she silently let herself be rolled around the room for fully fifteen minutes.

When she heard the clock strike, she rose, but kept the bottle firmly in her hand. This day she wanted to take it home with her. Before leaving, she ran back once more to the table to put a handful of candy into her pocket. Seeming somewhat distracted, she then left the room without a word.

9

"Don't look as if I wanted to kill you!"

It was Friday, and I was expecting Betty. When she arrived, with hardly a greeting, she placed herself in front of me, her hands on her hips, "Again you're not wearing pants! Why not?"

"I like myself better in a skirt," I replied. She walked past me, laid herself over the board of the swing, and letting her head, arms and legs dangle, she began to spit on the floor again and intensified this expression of her disgust with "ughs" and "blecchh's". After awhile she sat upright in the swing and said, "I like myself better in a skirt, too." She was swinging restlessly and then burst forth, "But my Mommy, she always forces me to put on pants!" She looked at me.

"Yes," I said, "and then you get angry."

"And how!" she confirmed, "but you can't even defend yourself against that."

"It must be bad, if there's no way to defend yourself against something like that," I returned.

She stopped swinging and rushed to the table. But she didn't like any of the sweets that day and pushed them all aside in disgust. She seemed listless and undecided.

Handing me a sheet of paper and a pencil, she said, "Now write down everything I would like for the next hour!" She dictated, "A hundred lollipops is what I want: ten green, ten yellow, ten red, and ten blue ones." To this she added, "You always have to write out the number ten, that makes it longer." I did everything as she said. When the sheet was filled, she took a satisfied breath. "Now, and you'll buy all that for me for next time?"

"Not everything, Betty. But now I know what you like, and next time you will find some of it on this table."

"Well, fine," she said, standing up and heading for the sandbox. "Come over here," she called, "let's make mud-pies. I feel like making mud-pies today."

While probing around in the sand, she asked me: "Do you know what a hedgehog is?"

"Of course I do."

"Is it true that it can pull its head under its spine completely?"

"Yes," I replied, "it can roll itself up completely."

Musing on this, she tried to curl up like a hedgehog and concluded, "How lucky. If it succeeds, if it can pull its head in completely, then it is all safe." She looked up at me.

"Yes," I answered, "for a hedgehog, that is important. That is its only means of defense. Other animals have different means of defense."

She tried to figure out how various animals defended themselves. "The rabbit can run real fast, birds can fly, the owl can see in the dark." Then she arrived at the helpless observation, "But people can't do any of that."

"No, they can't, Betty. But man, too, has his own means of defense."

She was silent. I knew we had hit upon a problem which—for her—could not be solved by words. She picked up some clay and formed a crocodile with a large jaw in which she shaped sharp, pointed teeth. Then she dipped her hands into the finger-paints and drew a wolf running to the right, its jaws wide open, and with long white teeth. Suddenly she exclaimed, "I have to go to the bathroom immediately! Come with me!" Having settled down there, she made a most pertinent remark, "Funny, every time I'm at your house, I have to go to the bathroom. That's because it's so cozy here."

These toilet-scenes were obviously pleasing to her. Through them she was unconsciously making up for something she had missed during her anal stage. As usual, there were her accompanying comments. "First you pee, then come the sausages. The sausages of big dogs are bigger than those of little dogs." She had long finished her business, but remained seated in a state of gratification and seemed to delight in the odor. She made her wishes known. "Why don't we knead and form things right here. At home I just made a butt with clay." She went on talking merrily: "Did you ever see my butt?" When I said no, she returned, "Well, and I haven't seen yours, either."

"Okay," I said, "why don't we each mould our buttocks with clay."

She liked that idea. Immediately she jumped up, ran ahead of me into the therapy room, and kneaded her buttocks in no time. I did the same. Snickering, she then hurled both our buttocks firmly onto the floor. She rubbed her hands clean and stood up straight. "You know what I said to my Mommy?"

"Well, no. How should I know that?"

She giggled softly. "I said, today I'll tell Mrs. Ude to sit on the potty here in the room and make something in it."

She looked at me challengingly.

"And that would please you?" I returned.

Suddenly she tore the silk scarf from my neck and tucked it into my belt.

"Now, you leave that there!" she yelled, "And sit down quietly right here and don't budge!"

She stood before me with her fingers forced apart, hulking over me.

"I see you want to play fighting with me," I said, emphasizing the word "play" in order to remind her of her limits. I proposed a wrestling match which she readily accepted. I gave her a good fight, but in the end left her with the impression that she had wrestled me down.

The match calmed her for the moment. She ran to the stove to cook, as she said, "something delicious for Sebastian and her Mommy," who were coming to pick her up. As before, she indiscriminately poured heaps of ingredients into the bowl. Stirring the concoction, she frequently glanced at me with flashing eyes. I had to sit on the couch as if petrified and was not to budge from that spot. Now and then she gave orders, asking me to hand her this or that. But every time I had to return to my seat immediately. When I lightly touched the rocking-horse standing next to me, at once she came running to me furiously. "You only want to annoy me!" she screamed. "You're stupid; a stupid ass, a real dummo; my Mommy isn't as stupid as you are!"

With her fingers spread tensely, she stood before me like a wildcat ready to scratch my eyes out. Seething with hatred, she screamed at me, "I hate you, I hate you, I hate you!"

She fled to the swing. Her face was marked with hatred and despair, perhaps the most depressing expression one could ever see on a child's face.

Then she said, "Don't look as if I wanted to kill you." Lying face down over the swing with her arms, head, and legs hanging limply, she swung back and forth for a considerable while, before she began to sing softly, "I'm flying, I'm flying and I'm not getting wet." She repeated this several times. I hummed along, and slowly she regained control of herself.

When the mother came with Sebastian to pick her up, she ran toward her with the same anxious outcry as in her first session, "Mooommy, Mooommy!" Betty pulled her mother and Sebastian back into the playroom. Her mother asked, "What did you do today?"

Hesitating, Betty answered softly, "Look, I cooked something good for you."

Mrs. Bonsart turned to me. "Is that all she did,

cook?" I did not answer, but was relieved when the mother tasted Betty's cooking, although she did it with cool reserve.

I said good-bye. Mrs. Bonsart stayed another few minutes with her children in the playroom.

Later, when I was tidying up, I came upon a large envelope containing a note by Betty's mother: "Dear Mrs. Ude . . . Enclosed is Betty's latest drawing . . . Cordially yours, Mrs. Bonsart."

(Picture 15) A huge, frightful colossus reminiscent of a dinosaur wallowed from right to left. The monster's head and neck, however, were turned to the right.[1] In the gaping mouth one saw sharp, yellow teeth and an extended fiery tongue. The conspicuous black line, splitting the large green eye in half, emphasizes the torn, conflicting feelings expressed in this picture: flight and attack, fear and aggression. The colors, too, were expressive of an entire range of emotions: Violet, which is predominant in this picture, is the color of mourning, of mysticism. There is a frightening chill in the poisonous-green of the eye. As all colors, the glaring red of the tongue has two meanings: Red is the symbol of love and warmth, but it is also the symbol of turmoil and blood; of deviltry and scorching fire.

The mighty weight of the animal's body, writhing from right to left, pointed to a still dangerous blockage of aggression. But with the right turn of the dinosaur's head, Betty's creativity had im-

[1] See also page 11.

pressively illustrated the positive therapeutic result of the dramatic incident in which she had wanted to "kill" me.

For me this marked the apparent initiation of a promising psychic process in Betty: her blocked aggressions, which hitherto had been self-destructive, were being redirected toward the outside world.

A Call from Lisa

The following Tuesday my telephone rang. Lisa, the Bonsart's live-in baby-sitter, called to excuse Betty from her therapy hour. Betty was ill with a fever.

"Did she catch a cold?" I asked.

"No," Lisa replied, "it doesn't seem to be a cold; we don't know what is causing her fever."

I wished Betty a speedy recovery and asked Lisa when it might be possible for me to reach Mrs. Bonsart by phone to make an appointment for a talk with her alone. Lisa explained that Mrs. Bonsart was on a trip, but that she was expected back for Betty's first day of school. That would be very soon, since school was to start in three days.

We agreed that I be notified by phone as soon as Betty was able to continue her therapy.

A Call from Betty's Mother

I had not heard from Betty's family for a week when Mrs. Bonsart called to report that Betty's fever had dropped quickly and that she had been able to enter school five days before. "School is a catastrophe," Mrs. Bonsart said, "I'm dismayed. Today I spoke with her teacher; she doesn't know what to do with Betty. Betty reportedly is wrapped in total silence, sits at her desk, as if paralyzed, and doesn't say a word.

"I briefly told the teacher of Betty's therapy with you, but it might be good if you spoke with her, too. Perhaps then they'll show more understanding for Betty at school."

The teacher's name was Mrs. Sibilsky. Mrs. Bonsart had already looked up her telephone number, and I promised to get in touch with her right away. We also fixed a date for our first talk, which was to be in three days.

Telephone Conversation with Betty's Teacher

I was fortunate to reach Mrs. Sibilsky at my first try. She was grateful for my call, since she was deeply concerned about Betty. "It's as if Betty were there in body only. Inwardly she seems completely numb and frightened. She doesn't say a word, dares not raise her hand or make the slightest move. I myself am reluctant to address her, because she gets terrified and freezes instantly.

"The other children like her, but they treat her like a baby. The girl next to her takes out the note-books and pencils for Betty from her satchel and whispers to her, telling her what to do. If the other children weren't leading her out into the school yard and back into the classroom again, Betty would not leave her desk at all.

"What can I do with this child?"

I told Mrs. Sibilsky about Betty's therapy, trying to give just a broad picture of it, and was much relieved to find that she had an understanding for the enigmatic nature of the unconscious. Her insight into these matters became apparent when she talked about her pupils' drawings.

"During art period I asked the children to draw a princess," she said. "They eagerly pursued the assignment and painted the most beautiful pictures. But not Betty. She drew her princess as a skeleton with large hollow eyes. That shocked not only me but the entire class."

Mrs. Sibilsky then told me that she had deliberated as to whether or not Betty should be held back from school for a year. She was reluctant to do this because the next year Betty would be too old for the first grade and might develop new inferiority complexes which would only be an additional burden to the child.

We agreed that Mrs. Sibilsky would keep Betty in her class, but that she would leave her completely alone for the time being. After half a year, she then planned to sit down with Betty in order to judge whether or not Betty had absorbed any of the material, whether she had learned to read, and to evaluate Betty's intelligence in general. I was glad to learn that Mrs. Sibilsky would have Betty's class for two years. Mrs. Sibilsky asked for my telephone number in order to be able to discuss with me any problems which might arise.

10

"I hate you, I hate you . . ."

Lisa brought Betty for the next session. As Betty ran ahead into the playroom, Lisa handed me a large envelope with a picture by Betty. Meanwhile Betty was sitting at the table, sucking on a root beer lollipop. "You must have known that I needed these lollipops very badly today, that's why you didn't forget them."

"Yes, and you haven't been here for a week. Much has happened in the meantime."

She propped her head in her hands. After some time she declared, "It's wonderful to be here all alone with you." She nodded, licking her lollipop. Then she asked, "What was the name of your teacher in school?"

"My teacher's name was Miss Nölle." Betty chuckled briefly. "What a funny name! My teacher's name is Mrs. Sibilsky. Was she nice, Miss Nölle?"

"Sometimes yes, sometimes no," I answered hesitantly.

"Mrs. Sibilsky is quite nice," Betty remarked casually. Then she looked up at me with wide questioning eyes, "Did you like going to school?"

I shrugged my shoulders. "Sometimes yes, sometimes no."

"You didn't like it either?" Betty perked up. "And why not?"

I made my answers reflect her own problems. "Because sometimes I was a little afraid in school."

Betty wanted to hear more. "And you didn't raise your hand either?"

"No," I replied, "in the beginning I never did."

"And you also didn't say anything?"

"No, only very little."

"You know what," said Betty excitedly, "in my class there's a mute girl, too."

"She can't speak?" I asked.

"Why, yes, she can speak—but then again she can't speak."

"Yes, that can happen," I said and repeated her sentence, "Sometimes one can speak, but then again one can't speak." Betty had to laugh a little about this. Then she asked, "How were the other kids with you?"

"Oh," I said, "they were quite nice to me, but they always treated me like a baby, took me by the hand to lead me out of the classroom or got the books out of my satchel for me—"

Betty interrupted me, "And that annoyed you and made you angry, didn't it?"

"And how!" I assured her.

"And what did you do?"

"One day I just told them firmly, 'I don't want you to treat me like a baby, I'm as big as you are!'"

Betty beamed. "That's good. But you could have gone to Miss Nölle, too, and told her about it."

"No," I said, "I didn't want to do that. I finally asserted myself."

With that, the subject of school seemed closed for the time being. Betty wandered about the room, unable to make up her mind. She swung a little and then decided on the sandbox. Seemingly relaxed, she stuck her hands deeply into the sand and let it trickle through her fingers. I was kneading some clay. In a totally abstract form Betty suddenly recognized a crocodile. "That's a crocodile," she said. "Make more of those."

After the third one, she wanted me to make a very big crocodile. When they were all finished, she scrutinized them, and observed, "But none of them have teeth. They do need teeth, so they can bite people." I agreed, and together we placed teeth into the crocodiles' jaws. Betty picked up the large crocodile with both hands and wielded it about, exclaiming in a curt and abrupt manner, "Haw, haw, haaaw, now everybody is afraid of me." But in the next moment she said to the crocodile in a hissing voice, "That's enough of you." She went to get the crocodile from the puppet theater. "This one has extra sharp teeth." She made the puppet-crocodile bite and hack the clay-crocodile to pieces, "into a thousand shreds."

Betty took genuine pleasure in this "murder" of the crocodile. What was left of it, she crushed with her hands. Obviously satisfied, she went to the sink to wash. There she discovered a bottle of nail polish. "My mother says that's only for women; little girls would look ugly with it." She looked up at me.

"Still, maybe little girls would like to try it," I suggested.

Eagerly she applied polish to her nails and seemed pleased with the result. I was sitting close by on a little stool. Betty looked at herself in the mirror. "You combed your hair differently today," I remarked, "you parted it in the middle. That's pretty on you."

Her voice became sharp. "Ah, you're just saying that; my Mommy told me she didn't like this hair style." Betty continued to study herself in the mirror. Suddenly she also discovered my face in it and yelled into the mirror, "Stop that stupid laughing!" She instantly turned around, reached for her wool cap, and in a flash pulled it over my face, as if wanting to suffocate me with it. Taking off the cap I could see a shocking expression of hatred and despair appearing on her face. She beat against my chest with her fists, "I hate you! I hate you!"

I remained totally passive. My face showed neither fright, nor anger, nor a smile. This was not mere patience on my part; rather my attitude stemmed from the deep understanding of emotional phenomena which I had gained during my professional training. A wrong reaction at this moment would either bring this needed therapeutic process to a standstill or it would leave Betty feeling guilty and confused, depriving her of a desperately-needed opportunity to externalize her severe inner conflicts.

With an outcry she fled into the armchair where she curled up. After a while she asked for the baby-bottle.

"Push me around," and I again pushed her through the room. She was still curled up in the armchair when she heard the voice of her mother, waiting outside. She protested, "No I don't want to stop yet. My Mommy always comes when I don't want her to, but she doesn't come when I need her." But snatching a handful of candy, mechanically she left the room.

I immediately sat down at my typewriter to write up a report of this session. First I opened the envelope Lisa had given me at the beginning of the hour. It contained a drawing (picture 16) by Betty: a girl whose mouth is blotted out by large black circles. The girl is Betty herself, the mute girl in her class. The black circles over the mouth symbolized Betty's inability to speak in school.

11

"Betty always was a difficult child; with Sebastian it was easier from the start."

For what was to be one of our many talks, Mrs. Bonsart arrived fifteen minutes late. She said things had been very hectic; still her appearance was immaculate. She used good judgment in dressing and adding stylish touches.

Mrs. Bonsart immediately began to talk about Sebastian who was ill with a fever and who was worrying her, especially since it had not been possible to get him to take the prescribed medicine. She told how she and Lisa had held the boy down with all their might just to administer some medicine, in spite of his fierce resistance. Betty had also witnessed this procedure which had upset her as much as it had the two women.

When I expressed my doubts about such brutal measures, Mrs. Bonsart admitted that this indeed had gone beyond her strength. For this reason she had taken Sebastian that morning to the pediatrician to let her administer the medicine to the boy. The pediatrician wrapped Sebastian in a blanket so that his arms and legs were immobilized; only in this way was it possible to give him the medicine.

However, Mrs. Bonsart said, his screaming was frightful. "But, now," she said, "he is fine. The fever is already gone; the medicine must have done some good." I remarked that this "professional" approach to the problem surely was an assault on Sebastian. Mrs. Bonsart belittled the importance of this event: "But he has long forgotten that."

"Perhaps he did forget," I returned, "but the crucial point is that his fear and all his feelings connected to this incident remain stored in the brain for life. Traumas (literal meaning: injuries) experienced as a child serve as basic models or precedents for a person's later behavior. Subsequent experiences, which in themselves may be only trifles, can recharge themselves with suppressed, 'forgotten' traumas and can trigger the same dramatic fears as the actual traumatic incidents."

Here I had touched upon a problem in Mrs. Bonsart's own life. She said, "I've been told that when I was a child of a year and a half, I accidentally was locked into a dark bathroom. Now I'm terrified of overly narrow rooms and even of closed rooms in general." After a while she recalled that she felt oppressed in trains as well.

It was an especially beautiful autumn day. The turning of the leaves was at the height of color. We sat next to each other at a large window so that we did not look at one another directly. This created a freer atmosphere and made it easier for us to accept the long periods of silence.

Mrs. Bonsart said quietly, "This display of fall colors is like a euphoric glow; like the prelude to requiem."

"You see it as such?"

She did not respond. Abruptly she began to talk about Betty. "Whatever can you say to Betty? How is it possible that she utterly stops functioning at school, withdraws into herself, doesn't speak, remains timidly at her desk during recess. That certainly can no longer be considered normal. She must be congenitally afflicted and will therefore by nature always develop new problems."

I recalled our first conversation where we could not find in the histories of either family any factors indicating a congenital source to Betty's problems. The report of the neurological examination had also been "without evidence."

"It's hard to get along with Betty," Mrs. Bonsart continued, "with her stubbornness and her hysterical fits. She is so mean to her brother, and is frighteningly devoid of feeling."

"I can well understand," I sympathized, "that it's hard for you to endure Betty as she is now."

"But I know," she suddenly remarked, "what my main pedagogical error is. I am too lenient, Mrs. Ude; Betty's tenacity is often so exhausting to me that eventually I simply must give in."

"Give in? When, for instance?" I was surprised.

"Well, for instance, in questions of dress. Betty never wants to wear what I consider to be right. Every morning, again and again, there is a fight between us."

"And why is it so hard for you to let Betty decide for herself what to wear?"

"I simply want her to look nice," she replied with an air of self-confidence.

"And you think, Mrs. Bonsart, that Betty looks less pretty in the clothes she selected herself?"

"Yes, I think so. She cannot wear everything. Perhaps—it may be—that I am particularly fastidious and demanding in questions of taste."

"Betty is unquestionably a pretty girl," I interjected, "and she is exceptionally well-built besides. Even the ugliest clothes couldn't change much about that."

"But Betty must realize after all that I only mean well, that, in trying to dress her nicely, I only want her to look her best."

"Your intellect, Mrs. Bonsart, leads you to think that Betty must realize this, but Betty feels very differently about it."

"Why? What do you mean?"

"Well, Betty must have the feeling that she is not being loved and accepted as she is. She probably experiences your continual criticism of her clothes as a rejection."

Mrs. Bonsart could not accept this view. "But, you see, it's mainly Betty's manner, her character which gives me so much trouble. She has always provoked me; with Sebastian it was easier from the start. Betty always was a difficult child. Just yesterday I went through a battle with her. We were buying shoes. Betty insisted on getting ugly red patent leather shoes. She behaves in such an hysterical way. She is so overly girlish on the whole that I can't stand it."

I let her statement rest a while.

Then I took over the direction of our conversation. "From your viewpoint, I can understand you very well, Mrs. Bonsart. To you, Betty is living out a role which you did not want to, or rather could not accept: the role of a girl."

"I know," she said after a moment. "Betty would love to make me into a bosomy mama. But I cannot change. Neither can I engage in childish play with Sebastian, as it no doubt would be good for him. Besides I did not play with dolls as a child." Mrs. Bonsart talked about her childhood, about her extremely cool relationship with her father, about the fears she experienced when she accidentally was locked into a dark bathroom, about threats of gypsies taking her away, of the frequent moving from city to city, and about her painful smallness as a girl. Again she recalled how hateful the laughter of the other girls had been to her, when the teacher had simply lifted her up like a doll, exhibiting her to the class. At that time the wish grew in her to be a big boy like her brother who, because of his size and strength, supposedly was able to get along more easily with his surroundings. Finally she made this comment.

"It is now firmly engraved upon my soul that I must always assert myself, must always fight with my intellect, and in doing so, I must always go beyond my strength."

"I can understand that very well, Mrs. Bonsart.

When your feelings are severely hurt in your childhood, you must repress them with your intellect, because after all you want to live. Man cannot live with constant pain."

Mrs. Bonsart returned to Betty once more, "What makes her hate her little brother so much? What makes her so vicious and rough with him that I often truly fear for Sebastian's safety?"

"There is a drawing by Betty, in which she touches upon exactly this problem." I gave this drawing (picture 17) to Mrs. Bonsart for a closer examination.

About this picture Betty had remarked, "The big dog's name is Jaggy, he is not on the leash and that's why he's crying. And the little dog is Bunny; he is still leashed to the corner store." This drawing is an unconscious, yet clear account of the source of Betty's jealousy.

Here Betty conveys a problem—which otherwise would call for long explanations—simply with three figures: the two dogs and the corner store. Once one understands their symbolic meaning, the interpretation of this picture is obvious. The big, crying dog without a leash is Betty; the small dog, Sebastian, and the corner store stands for a source of nourishment, of plenty. In a store one can get everything, as from a mother. It therefore symbolizes the mother. The leash ties the small dog to the store, that is, to the mother. He still lives in close contact with her, whereas the big dog is no longer leashed to the store. Therefore he feels deserted, forlorn, and alone and turns away crying.

It is interesting, too, that the close tie between the store and the small dog is accented by their having the same color, whereas the big dog is of another color.

Mrs. Bonsart readily accepted my interpretation of this picture, adding affectionately, "The little dog does look like Sebastian, he has the same tousled mop of hair." After a period of strained silence, she asked, "Whatever can I do to make Betty feel less rejected?"

I deliberately left this question unanswered. What good would it do, if the mother now tried to suppress her criticism of Betty's clothes, but could not change her basic attitude toward the child? Then a resigned indifference might take the place of the former struggle with Betty, which would make the child feel even more forsaken.

The way to a lasting solution was for Mrs. Bonsart to confront her own self and then gradually change her unconscious attitudes. Not only the child, but the mother as well had a right to demand patience. For Mrs. Bonsart—with her reactions firmly established over many years—psychological change was even more difficult to achieve.

Our conversation came to an end. Almost abruptly Mrs. Bonsart took her leave. "I shall call you again. Next week I'm going to Paris for a few days. A little trip like that always relaxes me."

As I walked her to the door, she handed me a drawing (picture 18) by Betty. Smiling a little, she remarked, "Today it is something specially large."

On two large sheets of drawing paper, glued together, Betty had drawn a giant crocodile with a solid row of protruding teeth. It was the puppet-crocodile from our last session, which, as Betty had said herself, had bitten my clay-crocodile into a thousand shreds. In contrast to her previous monsters, this one moved from left to right.

At the door I asked the mother whether Betty still showed self-destructive tendencies such as beating her head on the floor and tearing out her hair. She said she had observed neither for some time.

Betty's pent-up aggressions must have found new outlets in therapy.

12

"Today I must recover at your house."

Apparently Betty had come directly from school to her therapy hour. She looked very pale and hollow-eyed, walking wearily as if she had dragged herself to my house with her last strength. In the playroom, she let her satchel and coat simply slip to the floor.

"Today I must recover at your house," she said in a feeble voice and dropped herself face down over the swing. Rocking back and forth, she began to spit in disgust on the floor. After a while she stated, "It's all very bad."

"You mean school?"

She did not respond. I didn't push her. She would surely find her own way of expressing why everything was bad. Her head, arms, and legs hung down limply. Apparently this position and her constant spitting was her only way "to recover." This time it took particularly long for her to free herself from the swing. Listlessly she wandered to the table where there were always sweets. She pushed them aside with a brusque gesture. "Bleccchh!" Gradually her movements became more vigorous. She fetched a clump of clay for each of us. Probing in the soft mass, she began to form something. "So! Now I have a knife."

"That's for defending oneself, Betty."

"No, no," she protested anxiously, "that's only my handy-tool." She dipped her hands in the red finger-paint and smeared it on the blade. "That is blood red." Suddenly she dropped everything and ran to the sink where she went through a lengthy ritual of cleaning her hands. After that she went to the puppet theater, announcing, "I'll play something for you."

I was assigned to the rocking-horse. From the baby carriage, Betty picked up a small hand-made doll which had an especially sweet face and blond curls. "This will be the devil," she declared, pressing a pair of horrible clay eyes on the doll's face. It obviously gave her an inner satisfaction to press in eyes. Next she took out the two devil puppets. "I must make them still uglier," she said and pressed clay-eyes on them also, adding a thick nose and long teeth to each face. "These devils want all children to go and play in the street. Haw, haw, haw! All children get run over, they all get killed."

Then she fetched the crocodile. "More and more crocodiles are coming, they all are hungry and want to eat and gobble up the dead children." Finally she picked up Kasper and had him slay all the crocodiles. Betty gloated over this violent murder. Hiding behind the stage, she began to snicker and suddenly threw little pieces of clay at me, commenting, "This is an eye, this a nose, and this

84

a leg—" Tossing out these "torn-off" limbs was markedly gratifying to her.

"What next?" she said softly as if to herself. Her destructiveness apparently was not yet satisfied. "Shall I knock over the whole stage?" she whispered. Her lips were tightly pinched and her hands rigidly clenched in fists ready to strike out in all directions.

Then suddenly the whole puppet theater flew toward me. Fortunately I was able to catch it just in time so that she would not become aware of the chaotic nature of her action. A shattered puppet theater very well might have produced a harmful shock in her at this time, leading to crushing feelings of guilt. Betty looked at me with fierce eyes. "Today I would like to smear all over the walls."

"Not in here! Only in the next room, Betty!" (There was a windowless room next to the playroom where children could throw things against the walls.)

She hesitated and squabbled, objecting to this limitation. I remained firm. Disgruntled and without a word, she finally went to the other room. "And can I really smear all over these walls?"

"Here you can do whatever you like, Betty."

"Even smash this mud against the walls?"

"Even that."

Again she began to snicker. First she threw only little balls of mud against the wall, but instantly took courage, bombarding the walls with heavy, damp chunks. Whenever she hit upon wood, making an especially loud, sputtering sound, she opened her eyes wide. At last her strength flagged. The last mud balls barely reached their goal.

We returned to the playroom. Her agitated soul had temporarily found peace. "Let's sleep now, Mrs. Ude. I'll sleep here on the couch. And you on the floor." She took the soft pillow and the large cozy blanket for herself. To me she handed only a small towel. When I groaned that the floor was too hard, she snapped at me, "Go to sleep now, I don't want to hear another word!" She got up once more to fetch the baby-bottle and then "played" sleeping, but not for long. She soon began to talk, "Tell me, did you always say good morning to Miss Nölle?"

"Yes I did," I replied somewhat hesitantly. There was a silence. Then I asked, "How is the mute girl in your class?"

"She's still mute," Betty replied softly.

"Hm," was my only comment.

"Did the children in your class laugh at you, too?" she asked me.

"They did laugh sometimes, but that isn't necessarily making fun."

Betty burst forth, "But the children always laugh at me, I know they do! they're mean to me! it's so awful! Too bad," she continued, "that you're not strong enough, otherwise you could beat up all those kids."

"You don't feel strong enough to defend yourself?" Betty looked me straight in the face, but did not respond. I continued, "If one doesn't defend oneself, it gets worse and worse." And after a short pause, I added, "Because then one gets angrier and angrier at the other children." But Betty's stare was beyond me. Everything I said no longer reached her. Unconsciously she had switched off the communication. When I insisted with more "didactic" advice, she turned her head to the side. With that she silenced me. The remaining few minutes she stayed curled up on the couch with the baby-bottle in her arms. On this day she did not try to draw out our hour together, nor did she take any candy home with her. "Good-bye, Mrs. Ude," she said wearily and left.

The end of this hour made me think for a while. It was a reminder for me of one of the fundamental rules in psychotherapy: not to try to speed up the psychic process. Significant changes do not come from outside, but from within. And such counsel as I had just handed out was like dispensing formulas which to the child are meaningless. With such counseling communication breaks down and the child withdraws, as Betty had done just now. My "formula" read as follows: "You must defend yourself." Besides the fact that solutions coming from without counteract the autonomous process of maturation, my suggestion for Betty to defend herself was worthless, even wrong.

A child with a weak ego, a child who feels severely threatened by his inner fears will try to fight these off by projecting his hostility onto the outside world.

The child therefore perceives the frightening threats as if reflected in a mirror, coming from the outside.

A very small child, for instance, will pronounce the corner of a table as bad if he hurts himself on it. As the child matures, he must learn to retract such projections and to distinguish cause and effect.

As long as Betty's ego was so weak, she simply could not do without projecting her hostility upon an essentially friendly environment, since this brought her relief from inner tension. Therefore, if she were to act according to my "formula," if she were to defend herself, this would merely result in shadow-boxing.

13

"What will happen if you ever get ill?"

When Betty arrived for her therapy, I could not greet her as usual at the door. A telephone call had detained me for a few minutes. Utterly dejected, she was crouched on a chair when I entered the room. Disappointment was on her face. "You didn't look forward to my coming!" She looked up at me. Her eyes flickered restlessly like the eyes of a hunted animal.

"I'm sorry, Betty, that I'm late. I was on the phone." Together we walked into the playroom. Betty undertook nothing, remained standing rigidly, apparently unable to decide what to do.

We were silent for a while.

"Why were you on the phone so long? Aren't you a play-woman?"

"Even a play-woman must talk on the phone sometimes, Betty. You remember, you and I have talked before on the phone, too."

She did not stir. Then her great fear surfaced. "What will happen if you ever get ill? Or if you die? Are you going to die some day?"

"Everything that lives must die some day, Betty, but a person can get very old, seventy, eighty, ninety, or even a hundred years old."

"How long is that, a hundred years?"

"Well, let's think about that. First, how long is a year? A year has twelve months: January, February, March, April, May, June, July, August, September, October, November, December. That makes a year!"

She looked at me. "That is a long time."

"And now let's count how long one hundred years is: One year, two years, three years, four years, five years, six years."

"That's how old I am now."

"Yes, Betty." I went on counting: "Seven years, eight years, nine years, ten years, eleven years, twelve years, (Betty was counting along) thirteen years, fourteen years, fifteen years, sixteen years, seventeen years, eighteen years, nineteen years, twenty years."

"Is it still a long way to a hundred?"

"A very long way, Betty."

When I reached the count of thirty-five, she remarked, "And you still don't have to die?"

"No, Betty, and there are many more years before you get to a hundred."

With this, death seemed far removed to her.

She appeared relaxed and said, as she had so often before, "I have to go to the bathroom immediately." She fetched the potty, pushed it into a corner, and sat down on it. "It's so cozy here." She sat there for a while. Together we then emptied the potty in the bathroom, again Betty showing great interest in her excrement.

Back in the playroom she begged me, "I'd like to pet Cille! Please get Cille!" In petting an animal a child can rid itself of much tension and can receive much love in return. The only problem in this case was that Cille did not let herself be petted by children; she was jealous of them.

"Cille may gladly come, Betty. But she will disappoint you. She is jealous of all children."

"But I love her so much; please get Cille."

Cille reacted exactly as I had predicted. She immediately jumped on my lap and growled fiercely at Betty. Cille did not let her come near. Betty's every attempt to pet her was thwarted with frantic snarls and wild barking. Betty *was* disappointed.

Through the following conversation, however, it became possible to turn Cille's display of jealousy to a therapeutic advantage. I spoke only with Cille and told her that she need not be jealous of Betty, that she, Cille, was my very best, and that nobody could crowd her out. I noticed how Betty's expression changed, she seemed much more relaxed and was listening attentively. I continued to talk only to the dog, petting her lovingly. "Yes, you are my very, very best, I love nobody more than you." Then Betty joined in the conversation. She addressed Cille, "You don't have to be jealous, your mother loves you best in the whole world." I clearly sensed Betty's empathy toward Cille and how she identified with her jealousy. Betty then reproached me. "It's your own fault that Cille is jealous. Why did you get yourself another child?" With this she obviously meant herself. She went right on talking.

"When I was still all by myself in my Mommy's tummy, that was best of all."

"I can understand that, Betty. There you didn't need to share anything."

"Yes," she sighed. "Did you have a little boy when you were small?"

"You mean a little brother?" I asked.

"Yes. Did you have one, too?"

"Yes, I did."

"What was his name?"

"Michael."

"Hm, Michael," she said indifferently. "And what did he look like?"

"He had blond hair—" At once Betty interrupted me. "But Sebastian doesn't; he has brown hair. Did Michael scratch you sometimes, too?"

"Oh, yes, he did, sometimes."

"And did he always disturb you when you painted?"

"Oh yes, that too, Betty."

Now she banged her clenched fist on the table, startling Cille. "Just like Sebastian, exactly like Sebastian!"

And then, because she believed to have found in me a fellow sufferer, she fervently poured out her troubles about Sebastian. Again and again, she asked, "Did Michael do that, too?" Then she paused briefly. It seemed as if she wanted to ask a question which affected her more deeply. "And your mother, did your mother always defend Michael, too?"

"I often thought she did, but that wasn't true."

"But my mother!" Betty exclaimed, "She always

defends Sebastian; always Sebastian, only Sebastian."

"I sometimes imagined that, too, when I was a little girl, Betty."

"And how did the others treat Michael?"

"Ah, yes, they always found him especially cute, because he was so much smaller than I was."

"That's exactly how it is with Sebastian! Everybody—they all think he's so cute."

"That's only because he is so much smaller than you are, Betty. It's the same with animals."

She mused, "I, too, like the puppies and kittens best when they are real small." And she cupped her hands as if she were holding a tiny animal.

"You see, Betty, you feel that way, too."

After a while she asked, "But did your mother love you?"

"Yes, she loved me very much."

Betty folded her little hands and said almost devoutly, "My mother loves me very much, too, even though she scolds me."

"Yes, Betty, even if a person gets scolded at times, one still loves that person very much." (Nothing strengthens the self-confidence of the ego more than the certainty of being loved, and nothing crushes it more than the fear of not being loved.)

Cille still lay curled up in my lap. I had been rubbing her ears all this time, so that she would not disturb our conversation. And then our time was up. Betty quickly pocketed a handful of candy. As she left the room, she called back, "Good-bye, Cille, you jealous little puppy!"

A Call from Betty

On Tuesday the telephone rang very early. It was Betty. As she had done so often before, she had awakened that morning from a nightmare which was still vivid in her mind. Her grandmother's big dog, Arno, whom she loved so much, had split in half. One half was dead, the other half lived on as a cripple. Understandably, Betty was utterly disturbed by this dream which expressed her fear of falling apart, of splitting off from her real self. Through this dream the threat of this split had been projected onto the dog. "Help me, help me, Mrs. Ude, to stop this dreaming!" She could hardly put it into words, but her sobbing conveyed the agony she felt. However, after a few minutes she was able to ask me, "Can I come to see you right away? Please, please, let me come right now."

I had to tell her that this was not possible, but that she would be coming that afternoon at her usual hour.

"And when, when is that?" she wanted to know. She seemed to have lost all sense of time.

"Look at your hand, Betty. It's only in as many hours as you have fingers on one hand. Count your fingers."

She counted, "One, two, three, four, five." Already her voice sounded more cheerful.

"See you then, Betty, in five hours."

I put down the receiver without feeling worried. Betty had found the strength to contact me on her own.

14

"When the buds of the water lily open, a pretty girl will come out."

Without saying hello, Betty walked past me, sat immediately down at the table, emptied the jar of sweets, and idly moved her fingers through the little heaps of candy. "How long can I still come to see you?" was her first question.

"For as long as you like, Betty."

"Even when I'm a real big girl?"

"If you like, Betty, you may even come to see me then."

Betty detected a candle on the table, which a twelve-year-old boy had recently made for me. On one side of the candle he had painted flowers, on the other side a somber looking boy's face. He had commented, "Now I can turn the candle to either side, depending on how I feel, and then you know right away what's up."

Betty discovered the two sides on the candle: "It has a good and a bad side."

"Yes, Betty, good and bad, they're both a part of life."

She wanted to know who had made the candle. At once her jealousy was aroused. "Whom do you like better, Peter or me?" A straight answer seemed very important to her. Instinctively I replied, "I like you best of all."

Perhaps there was a therapeutically better answer, but I recalled a saying by Hermann Hesse: "I like him best who is with me."

Then Betty could think about playing again:

"You say what we want to play today," she asked me for the first time.

I made suggestions: "Let's play house—"

"Awful!"

"Let's paint or play with clay."

"No!"

"Let's play with the puppets."

"That's better!"

Meanwhile she had gone to the sink and let water run continuously into the little watering can. The water spilled into the sink, threatening to flood over onto the floor.

"Now I know what we'll play, Mrs. Ude. We're both on the great big ocean—there's nothing around us but water, water, water. We're sitting in a little boat, and the waves get bigger and bigger. And then we cry for help. Help! Help! But nobody hears us, the storm blows over us."

With dramatic gestures, she demonstrated the danger of being swept away by the waves. While calling out loudly for help, she emptied one can of water after another on the cement floor. When the boat was in danger of being swallowed up by the high waves, Betty ran to get Kasper. Now a giant crocodile emerged, threatening to capsize the

96

little boat. In a fierce struggle, Kasper killed the crocodile. The storm subsided and the sea gradually calmed.

Betty remained in her boat, splashing her hands around in the puddles. Then she stated, "Now the crocodile can live again, it'll just swim in the water and not eat any people, only fishes." (This was the first remark by Betty indicating that she had found a healthy basis for dealing with her aggressions. The crocodile, symbolizing her aggressions, did not get destroyed, e.g., the aggressions were not repressed, rather the crocodile was being put in its "proper" place.) She climbed out of her little boat and let ducks, fish, and a plastic water lily float on the water. Then she stretched out stomach down over the swing and exclaimed, "The ocean is wide and deep. I can see my face in it."

Full of joy she let herself swing "over the wide ocean" for a long, long time. She could hardly part with this game. Apparently it had a deeply soothing effect on her. She looked at the floating water lily and made a profound observation, "When the buds of the water lily open, a pretty girl will come out."

The hour was up. Betty filled her little purse with candy. At the door she turned around. "And don't forget how beautiful this game was."

A remarkable hour was over. How impressively she had acted out her previous dream, her fear of falling apart, by projecting that fear onto the threat of flood. Her final observation could have come out of a fairy-tale, "When the buds of the water lily open, a pretty girl will come out."

If one understands its rich imagery and enigmatic language, the fairy-tale is full of wisdom. The language of the fairy-tale emerges—just as dreams and play—from the unconscious and symbolizes the direction taken by the maturing personality. Seen in this light, Betty is unconsciously saying, "Once I have coped with my inner conflicts, I will emerge as a pretty, that is, healthy girl."

Hours such as this one are very gratifying to the therapist.

15

"What will happen, if a baby comes out?"

Betty arrived fifteen minutes late. She came into the room rather meekly and said, "My Mommy said that I should apologize to you."

"Apologize, because you are late? Well, that's not so bad, that can happen at times."

"Yes, that's what I told my Mommy, too. I said, 'Now don't get so upset; Mrs. Ude isn't that way at all.' My Mommy scolded the whole way and then, just when I got out of the car, she said to me, 'Well, now you go ahead to your Mrs. Ude, by all means.'" She imitated her mother's attitude and her voice.

Betty was wearing a Bavarian Dirndl dress that day. A thick wool sweater was sticking out from under her blouse. Looking down at herself she said, "My Mommy thought this was awful. But you, you like me this way, too. You don't nag all the time."

My way of listening sympathetically satisfied her for an answer, and she went on, "My Daddy told my Mommy already, too, 'Don't scold her so much.'"

She plucked at the sleeve of her sweater. "When I put this on, she said, 'For all I care, go ahead and wear that.'" Betty drawled out the words with a resigned attitude. Over her shoulder hung a little knapsack; she put it down and remarked, "In here are ghosts, crabs, and spiders which I cast myself." She put them on the table, stretched the leg of a spider until it tore off, and commented with an expression of horror and ecstacy, "Oh! I like to do this so much!" Then suddenly she looked at me with fierce eyes and shoved me aside.

"Go away!" she yelled at me. "Don't laugh so stupidly! You probably think I'm a witch! You don't love me!" She was overcome with despair. She threw herself into the corner of the sofa and screamed: "Say that you love me! Say now that you love me!"

And as I had so often before, I assured her that I loved her very much. "No matter how you are, Betty, whether you are good or bad, happy or sad, I always love you."

Now other questions came again. "Do you find the children in my class stupid?"

"I do not know the children in your class, Betty."

"But if you knew them, would you like them?" She was beating the pillow with her fists. "I don't want you to like them!"

"I also would like them, Betty. The more children one loves, the more one can love a single child—you, Betty."

She remained silent, but had calmed down. Looking at my white boots, she mused, "Today I saw somebody with white boots in town, and I thought that must be you."

"You, then, looked forward to this hour with me; just as I always look forward to this hour with you?"

"Yes," she repeated, "I look forward to it so much, to see you again."

She now turned her interest to the finger paints and declared pink to be her favorite color. "You know," she said, "I don't need the other colors anymore, I only need pink. All I want to paint with is pink." While she was spreading the pink paint over the sheets, she talked about Arno, her grandmother's dog. "With Arno I can do everything I want to. He is big and strong; after all, he's a man; and Cille, the jealous one, is small and saucy; she is a girl."

"Yes, that is probably the way it is," I said.

Suddenly fear appeared on her face again. "But what would Cille do if an evil man pierced her tummy and sucked out blood?"

It was the same question she had asked in one of the earliest sessions.

A few days earlier Betty had drawn a picture which touched upon the fear expressed in her question. It showed a dog with long ears like Cille's. The teats identified it as the body of a female dog. A red form easily recognized as a penis penetrated the female body (picture 19).

I felt that now was a good time to use this picture in dealing with her question. "You asked once before 'What would Cille do, if a bad man shoots arrows into her tummy?'" Betty remained silent.

101

"Somewhat like this picture where something like an arrow is shooting into Cille's body," I prodded further.

She did not respond. She was totally unconscious of the fear that had brought on her question. "But the arrow doesn't look like an arrow at all. It could also be something which every boy and every father has."

"A peepee," Betty said spontaneously.

"Yes, a peepee, Betty, is not an evil arrow and doesn't stab into a tummy and doesn't suck out blood."

Suddenly she jumped up and shouted, "I have to go to the bathroom in a hurry! Come with me!" On our way there, Betty asked, "What will happen if a baby comes out?" She sat on the toilet and strained. I explained to her that she could not have a baby yet, for that she would have to be much bigger, and that babies don't come out of the anus, anyway.

She was silent.

"From the anus the food wastes which the body cannot use are eliminated. And for the baby there is another opening, called the vagina."

"Yes," she said, "I know where that is; in front of the anus. But how can a baby come out there? That opening is much too small."

I explained to her that during delivery the vagina opens like a door, then the baby can readily slip out.

She began to giggle a little and said, "Up here," she pointed to her mouth, "I put something in and down here it comes out again. Up here I pour in water and down here it comes out again."

After she had repeated this several times, I said, "Only with a baby it is different. It slips into the same door from which it will come out again."

In answer to this Betty said, "And every boy and every Daddy has a peepee and from it sperm comes into the mother's stomach."

"That's right," I said, "When the Mommy and the Daddy love each other very much, then the sperm comes into the body of the mother and then a little child is born."

Although Betty had long finished her business, she did not want to leave the toilet. I felt as if she still wanted to tell me something. Her face showed a slight, nervous twitching. "I must tell you something. Yesterday I went to the sauna with my Daddy again. He said, 'You're my little wife.' Then another man and a woman came into the sauna. The man was awfully fat. I couldn't see his peepee. But then, one shouldn't make fun of anybody in the sauna. I went back into the sauna with Daddy over and over again and then back into the cold water. Afterward all the cots were taken by the other people. Only one was free, and Daddy and I had to lie down on it together."

She was silent.

"That is," I said simply, "a big Daddy-man was lying with his little wife on the bed, and both were completely naked."

Betty pondered a while and then said, "My Daddy is married to my Mommy, but I often go to the sauna with Daddy, and we sometimes also sit in the bathtub together."

"You're right," I said, "your Daddy is married to your Mommy. But when little girls are as old as you are, they would like best to marry their Daddy, too. But when the girls grow up, they find their own husbands whom they love and marry."

After this conversation, she became withdrawn again. We remained together in silence. Betty merely remarked how cozy it was to be sitting with me in the bathroom. With much interest she then looked at her "big business." "Ooooh, how it stinks!" she cried and ran back to the playroom. It was clear that she still wanted to play.

She decided to work with the clay. After she had rolled a thick piece of clay for a while, she commented, "This is an earth worm." She pressed it flat, kneaded it to a long roll again, and put it into an open box with one end hanging over the edge. Then she slammed the cover over it so that the worm broke in half. She giggled. Then she suggested, "Why, the worm could crawl into somebody's anus, maybe yours? Or why don't you let him crawl into the doll's anus?" With that she doubled up laughing.

"It would make you happy if the worm crawled into a body?" I asked casually.

Next she kneaded a "very, very, large earth worm." "That now is the Daddy earth worm," she declared. She wielded it about as if she wanted to frighten me by it.

Then she formed many little clay worms which

were to crawl over the body of the Daddy worm. She lifted the Daddy worm and said tenderly, "But this is Daddy," and kissed it.

"You like the Daddy worm."

"But the real earth worms, the ones in the garden, I don't like to touch them, they squirm around my fingers and don't let go of me." She shook her fingers, "Ugh, I am afraid of them."

"Sometimes you are afraid of earth worms and then you like them," I observed. "Sometimes you want them to crawl over a body and then again they are evil arrows to you."

She looked at me. "Evil arrows from evil men."

"Yes," I said, "like on this picture."

In silence we then looked at the dog picture (picture 19) for a short while. With that we had reached the limit of the interpretation of her unconscious fear. She fetched the baby-bottle again and sat down in the swing with it. Swinging gently, she said: "I am soooo tired." Her eyelids became heavy. Then she made the remarkable comment, "You are my play-helper. Other people might think you are my Mommy."

"Yes, Betty," I repeated, "I am your play-helper."

Although the clock had announced the end of her hour, she did not want to leave yet. "Just once, I would like to sleep at your house for a whole night. Please, please!"

But then, with a handful of candy she marched off after all.

Once more the past hour clearly revealed the intensity of Betty's unconscious sexual fears, her fear that a penis could enter into her body. This fear she had conveyed dramatically in several drawings previous to picture 19: picture 6, "Big ghost bites into child's blood;" picture 7, "Girl's head with mice and spiders;" picture 13, "Sun with evil fingers," as well as in the following picture which she had drawn before entering therapy (picture 20).

Picture 20 is divided into two parts by a black line. A girl with a penis and chopped-off arms is standing on the left. She is closed in on both sides by sharp spikes pointed at her. On the right hand side of the picture is a man—more ghost than man, a ghost in a bottle—with an eye on each side of his head. From the many little bottles and the clearly discernable tooth brushes standing on the shelves, one can assume that this is a bathroom scene. The girl's chopped-off arms, the frame of spikes, and the eyes demonstrate Betty's fear of punishment. The penis is either an expression of her penis envy or of her desire to protect herself: "then no one can penetrate me."

The same dramatic fear appeared in her nightmares: for example, in the one (see page 26) where Betty and her mother stand under a bridge, "And there was a black man," which is symbolic of the sensual, the erotic; "And he had very evil eyes," which symbolizes fear of punishment; or in her dream about the candle (see page 46).

Her play with the clay worm (phallic symbol) illustrated this fear as well, but it also brought out her affection and ambivalent wishes: she kissed

106

the Daddy-worm and let the little worms crawl over his body.

Betty was still living in the Oedipal stage which normally comes to a close at the age of five. The Oedipal stage is an important building block in the individual's development, starting around the age of three. During this time a child desires the parent of the opposite sex (healthy Oedipal complex), thereby assuming for the first time his appropriate sexual role. If the child does not meet with a supportive, pleasurable response during this time of erotic, sensual anticipation, his identification with this role can become confused. Therefore one can easily imagine that without the establishment of a positive Oedipal relationship at the right time, problems as an adult can result, for instance, difficulties of attraction to the opposite sex and of identification with the appropriate sexual role. With the Oedipal stage—just as with the preceding stubborn stage—a child encounters a flood of new emotions which he cannot cope with successfully without positive support from the parents.

If, however, the Oedipal tie to a parent is overly strong, and the relationship turns into a fixation from which the child cannot free himself, this may result in neuroses or perverse activities.

I believe it is sufficiently clear at this point that Betty had not yet overcome this problem.

16

"A substitute for love . . ."

In spite of his tight business schedule, Mr. Bonsart made himself available for the day's interview. When I offered him a cup of coffee, he also asked me for a lot of sugar. "I need a lot of sugar," he said, smiling a little, "a substitute for love. That's the psychological interpretation, right?"

"Yes," I smiled, "that may be."

Mr. Bonsart then began to talk at once about his family conflicts, how everyone got all wound up over trifles, and how one then found oneself trapped in a vicious circle. In this context he right away touched upon the power struggle which continued to exist between his wife and Betty, and which was kindled primarily by questions of dress. His wife, however, was seriously trying to avoid the problem.

About Betty he reported that she was still extremely difficult, but that her "hysterical" behavior had considerably toned down.

Then I spoke briefly about the various developmental stages of a child, pointing out especially the value of paternal assistance during the Oedipal stage. I mentioned that a highly sensitive child such as Betty would respond much more strongly to outer stimuli than a well-balanced child.

On his own Mr. Bonsart asked whether it was wrong that he took Betty to the sauna with him, that they sometimes sat in the bathtub together, and that Betty had once touched his penis.

I explained that such questions could not be answered simply with a yes or no, saying that the event in itself, as for instance, the communal bath, was not what counted primarily; but rather that the accompanying atmosphere, the underlying sentiments and the fantasies, which represent psychic realities, determined whether or not such intimate physical contact left traumatic impressions on a child.

Once more we looked at all of the pictures which most clearly conveyed Betty's fear of a "foreign" object penetrating a female body. The father was familiar with every one of these pictures, since it was he, who with almost pedantic care, had appended the date to each picture and had asked Betty for the meaning of each. After explanations of Betty's dreams and play in therapy, Mr. Bonsart was thoroughly convinced that a problem existed.

I explained that in his neurosis a child lives his parents' conflicts of which they themselves generally are unaware. A parent—in trying to overcome his disappointment in love, of which his own problems or a conflict with his partner may be the cause—may let some of his marital love enter into the relationship with his child. A child easily senses such subtle, unconscious fantasies of the parent concerned, and that, if continued over a longer period, could have a traumatic effect on the child.

As in the first interview with both his wife and himself, Mr. Bonsart again expressed his concern and awareness of how important a change in attitude by the parents was if Betty was to be helped. Although much remained unsaid in our interview that day, I still had the impression that we had touched upon deeper conflicts, helping the father see them more clearly.

Once more Mr. Bonsart spoke about his wife. Recognizing the correlation of past experiences with present reactions, he returned to his wife's childhood. Her father was a highly intelligent man, acknowledged as such among his professional colleagues. But he certainly had been of no real help to his daughter in her Oedipal stage. Mrs. Bonsart's mother had lived with cool reserve together with her husband who reportedly had been withdrawn and critical, hiding his feelings behind a brusque mask.

Most likely these were the reasons behind Mrs. Bonsart's reluctance to fully accept her feminine role. This, in turn, led to new conflicts with her spouse and children.

I then presented the father with H. E. Richter's book *Parents, Child, and Neurosis,* which deals primarily with the role of the child in the family. Using many examples, the author shows how parents, suffering from the pressure of their own conflicts, unconsciously try to force their child into

110

playing a role which will make it easier for them to endure their anxieties.

In his *Human, All-Too-Human,* Nietzsche had already recognized this phenomenon: "The unresolved dissonances—with regard to character and attitudes—in the parents' relationship forever resound in the child's being and make up the inner history of his suffering."

Before leaving, Mr. Bonsart handed me another picture which Betty had drawn at home on the day of her last therapy hour (picture 21). Referring to our first interview, Mr. Bonsart mentioned that Betty now painted comparatively little.

On the left, the picture shows a birth scene: the baby is tucked in swaddling clothes and is still connected to the mother by the umbilical cord. A black quadrangle frames the birth scene off from the other happenings. Below and to the right we see a red heart. Opposite the birth scene, on the right hand side of the picture, stands Death. If one looks closely, he no longer is as frightening as in the earlier pictures. He is dancing and wearing a fancy ribbon on his head. If we compare him to the former death figures, we find that he has lost his rigidity and merciless hold. It seems as if the wish for death was gradually being overcome. In the center of the picture the theme of birth is again touched upon; there is, among other things, an embryo and a baby. Life seemed to be gaining the upper hand.

But Betty was still a long way from lasting mental health, and we would most likely have to deal with relapses, since the origins of Betty's disturbances were implanted in the first days of her life.

At that point I pulled forth the notes of earlier interviews with the mother. Here are two excerpts:
. . . Mrs. Bonsart spoke again about the depression she experienced right after Betty's birth, in spite of hers and her husband's happy anticipation of the child. Yet Betty had not been neglected. Mrs. Bonsart said, "The child was a real comfort to me during that difficult time."

"If the baby was a comfort to you, then she gave you something, to be sure, but the question remains as to whether or not she received enough from you."

Mrs. Bonsart objected, "But the child perceives hardly anything during the first weeks."

"No, that is not right," I explained. "From the first day on, the emotional relationship between mother and child sets the pattern for the child's subsequent process of maturation. His entire development is crucially influenced by this first interaction between mother and child."

I asked whether or not Betty as a baby of six months and more had cried when a stranger bent over her bed. "Betty never cried; she responded to every stranger with a friendly smile," the mother replied confidently.

From six to eight months and on, a child must instinctively be able to distinguish the face of his mother (or nurse) from that of a stranger. Once a child has acquired this ability, he will be frightened and will cry at the sight of a strange face. The child's failure to cry must be considered a serious symptom. It indicates that the child has not been able to single out one individual to whom he can relate intimately as his source of happiness in life, and that therefore the child did not build up a basic reassurance and confidence in life and in his surroundings. In this case the infant has already fallen behind in his psychical development.

"And was it also significant that, until Betty was a year and a half old, or even longer, she called my husband and myself nothing but 'Daddy'?" Mrs. Bonsart asked me.

"Your depression certainly affected your vocal contact with the baby also. Therefore—what I would like to call—a tender cooing between mother and child probably did not develop, whereby the mother intuitively teaches the word 'Mommy' to the child by constant repetition."

An emotionally healthy and happy mother is abundantly rich in possibilities with which to communicate loving tenderness to the child by means of her body, beginning with breast-feeding, and by means of her hands, eyes, and her voice.

For this child to whom so much was denied in the earliest stages of her life, the healing process most likely still would require a long time.

17

"The whole world is poison. . . Let's create a paradise here for ourselves, which will last forever until we die. . ."

Another Tuesday had arrived and with it another hour for Betty. She seemed very sad that day. In her arms she was holding her "Linus blanket" and her favorite bear. She wanted to hide them at my house.

"Not in here," she objected, "where so many other kids come in, but in your other room where you are all by yourself." She hid her bear and her blanket in my bed. Visibly satisfied, she declared: "Now, everything here is safe, even from Sebastian."

In the playroom she was not interested in anything that day, neither the swing, nor sweets. She huddled in the soft armchair. "I am sad today," she said in a low voice. I nodded understandingly. She continued, "The whole world is poison." And then with an equally sad voice, "Let's create a paradise here for ourselves, which will last forever until we die. The windows shall never be opened anymore. This paradise belongs only to us until we die."

114

I was deeply disturbed by this relapse, but did not show it. I simply said, "Now you are a flower which wants to be covered by many snowflakes."

She looked at me with infinitely sad eyes. "Yes, make it snow." An intuition had made me place a large box of white wood shavings into the playroom that morning. This was wonderfully suited for "snow." I threw small handfuls of shavings into the air, which drifted gently to the ground as snowflakes in Betty's imagination. She wanted snow to cover everything.

Pointing at various objects, she directed me, "The swing. And now the little rocking-horse, the puppet-theater, the doll carriage." The whole playroom was being transformed into a snowy landscape.

Then the shavings—the snow—fell lightly over her entire body and her little face. "I am a flower and a blanket of snow is covering me."

I let this fantasy unroll very slowly. While throwing the snowflakes into the air, I let her experience her body by naming one by one which part the flakes would cover next, "The right leg, the knee." And on her face I mentioned every feature, the nose, the mouth, the eyes.

Thus this game gradually took on a childish nature, with the mother repeatedly asking, "And where is your little nose?" and the child tapping his finger at his nose, exclaiming blissfully, "Here!"

Her great sadness seemed slowly to fade, and she began to tell me how much she loved her mother: "I love my Mommy most of all, because she is my Mommy. But I love you most of all—" she instantly corrected herself— "After my Mommy."

The game had taken up the entire hour. As Betty walked out, she found a little twig. She gave it to me and said, "Next time we'll decorate it with Easter eggs." The Easter egg is a promising symbol, a symbol of growth and joyous anticipation. After regressing to the point of wanting to die, Betty found new strength for life.

18

"When you're dead, it's all over."

This particular day Betty came skipping in, dressed in an Indian outfit with a colorful sash tied around her hips.

She placed herself squarely in front of me, taking on an authoritative attitude, and said, "Huh! What is that you're wearing? Now, you put on a different dress immediately!" Her eyes flashed.

I grumbled that I did not feel like changing, and that I thought my dress was quite pretty.

"Pooh!" she protested and began rummaging in a box of children's costumes, material remnants, and ribbons. She brusquely tied a wide green ribbon around my waist.

"Now that looks better already." She remained standing before me, paused briefly, and then suggested, "Why don't we have a wrestling match?"

"Okay, Betty."

"But I am very strong," she warned.

"We'll see."

I made an effort to give her a hard match. Whereupon she said childishly, "Don't struggle so hard; I must win."

Lying on the floor, I became fully aware of the

threatening outbreak of her strong aggressions. I had to be alert. When she intimated, "You probably are afraid that I might hit you in the face with this stick." I quickly returned, "That's against the rules of our game. But one could draw a face on the blackboard."

She brought me some chalk. "Draw a face on the punching bag." I did it. Next she brought me some yellow chalk. "And draw the butt on the other side." After that Betty dipped her fingers in black paint and added a line to the buttocks. "That is the slit of the butt and that is the dumb butt hole." She poked it with her finger.

Next she poured her aggressions onto the punching bag. She scolded it. "You hit Sebastian! I'm going to get you for that!" She was hitting wildly at it with a large stick. "I'll poke this stick in your butt hole!" She spit at it, hitting it over and over with the boxing gloves, the handbrush, and the stick. Spitting continually, she yelled. "You got caca on your butt! Naughty, naughty! I don't want to see you anymore! I'll throw you in the garbage can; I'll flush you down the toilet; you'll get ground to pieces like Max and Moritz.[1] And then the animals will eat you up." She poured out an enormous repertoire of abuses and beat on and

[1] Translator's note: Max and Moritz are notorious little rogues who play tricks on petty bourgeois citizens, and who finally end up in a mill. They are ground to round seeds which form the outlines of their bodies. A flock of chickens picks them up one by one.

118

boxed with the bag until she was exhausted.

Afterward we both sat on a sheepskin on the floor.

She pointed at the punching bag, acting silly, and said, "That guy there is real goofy, isn't he?" I nodded. "But I'm good, I'm sweet and cute."

"That you are, Betty."

She repeated this game several times, each time moving a little closer to me. But she still kept her distance.

Children whose need for love and bodily contact has not been satisfied during infancy and afterward, often display a fear of touching and being touched. Whenever a vital need is not met, pain results. Since man cannot live with constant pain, he must suppress it. Later every act of tenderness, every caress tends to trigger this suppressed pain, and the individual builds up a fear of bodily contact as a means of avoiding this hurt.

I clearly sensed this fear in Betty—but at this moment I also sensed her longing for tenderness. She was in a conflict. I then tried to caress her by telling her why she was so cute. "Because of your beautiful brown eyes, your red mouth, your little nose, your hands—" She began to stretch out at ease, apparently enjoying this kind of tenderness.

With the green ribbon she had wrapped around my waist at the beginning of the hour, I then tried to establish bodily contact by using it to stroke, one by one, different parts of her body, always naming each. "That is the foot, and that is the leg—" After the ribbon had touched all parts of her body, she instructed me, "And now the face, and now the nose, the mouth—" In between she would warn, "But you don't touch me, only the ribbon."

"Only the ribbon will touch you," I reassured her.

The hate and aggression were gone from her face. She was completely relaxed. "You're happy, aren't you," she said, "to have a little girl like me."

"Yes, I am, Betty."

"I will always, always come to see you."

"For as long as you like, Betty."

"But you shouldn't have invited me to play, since you have such a jealous little Cille."

"Oh, well, one day she will understand that you don't want to crowd her out."

Betty sighed, "When one is dead, it's all over." She was silent for a while. She seemed to be growing more aware of her jealousy. "Cille is just as jealous of me as I am of Sebastian."

I repeated her sentence, "Yes, Cille is just as jealous of you as you are of Sebastian."

She switched to the topic of school. I asked about the mute girl.

"She isn't quite as mute anymore. But still you're always so alone—at recess and things—the other kids are different."

"Sometimes one simply feels different from the others," I suggested.

A sigh was her only response; apparently she

120

no longer wanted to discuss it. "Tell me a story," she begged.

The fairy-tale is a good aid in therapy. Selected correctly, such a tale can help bring about an awareness and sometimes relief of an emotional problem. At that moment I could not think of a suitable tale by Grimm or Anderson. So I called on my imagination. I told her a story about a little maid who tended a flock of geese on a bright meadow where flowers bloomed, and where fresh grass grew for the animals, where the flies hummed in the sun, and where a light breeze filled the air with the fragrance of herbs and flowers. Here the little maiden always settled down happily with her goslings.

". . . The young maid noticed that one gosling always wanted to sit right at her side and did not want to join the other goslings. The down of this gosling was of a different color than that of the others. It was white whereas all the others were yellow. And that is why it felt different and always huddled close to her. The maid was moved by this. One day she read in a big book that if one gathered yellow pollen, one could make the down of this gosling yellow as well. For many, many days she gathered yellow pollen, and when she had enough, she dusted the white gosling with it, whereupon it was just as yellow as the others."

Betty was relieved. "And then everything was well with the gosling."

"No," I continued, "That was just it. The little gosling could not believe that it no longer was different and kept on sitting sadly next to the maid." This story fascinated Betty. She looked at me expectantly, as I continued, "Then one day the maid placed the gosling among the others. At first it was afraid of them, then it noticed that the others only wanted to play and rub bills. The gosling slowly took courage, realizing that it was just like the others. It became happy again and played in the circle with the other goslings forever."

"Ah, I liked that story. And did the gosling really believe that it was yellow?"

"Yes," I answered, "once it had experienced that it was just like the others, it could always believe that this was true."

"The little maid must have loved the gosling very much," Betty said. "She helped it. She, too, was a helper."

"That must have been, Betty."

"Did she love the gosling just as much as you love me?"

"Just as much!"

As she was leaving the playroom, Betty said: "That was a beautiful hour. And next time you'll stroke me with the ribbon again and tell me another story like today."

Betty's Electro-Encephalogram

For days we had been expecting the results of Betty's electro-encephalogram. The parents had asked that the examination be given. The following incident was the reason for their action.

When Betty's mother had reprimanded her for her supposed untidiness, Betty reportedly ran into the kitchen, grabbed the bread knife, and dashed back with it into the livingroom where her mother was. Mrs. Bonsart was extremely upset over this incident, as she considered it a personal threat.

By means of the electro-encephalogram, including a general examination, and also for the sake of Sebastian, the parents wanted to find out whether or not this incident could be connected to possible brain damage in early infancy—a suspicion the parents had expressed to me before.

I opened the letter and read the results with relief. "Absolutely no indications of brain damage; merely a retardation of one year." The latter was not surprising in view of Betty's severe symptoms of phobias.

19

"Funny, you always know what I need so badly."

Betty looked rather depressed and pale the next time I saw her, and she wandered distractedly about the room. She pushed the candies off the table. "They stink, I don't like them." She began to spit on the floor again.

She got herself some clay. "I want to bake a ghost. It shall glow at night, and I'll hang it over my bed. Huuuugh!"

She tossed the clay aside, picked up some chalk, and drew a gigantic hollow-eyed ghost on the floor. "It doesn't matter, if I get dirty today, my Mommy is away on a trip again," Betty said when some chalk got on her dress. Still working on her horror-ghost, she went on talking, "When I get dirty, my Mommy scolds me, and then I always get afraid."

"But one cannot always be clean, Betty; when one is working, one gets dirty."

Monotonously she repeated my sentence, "One cannot always be clean; when one is working, one gets dirty." She drew another enormous phantom on the floor: a dinosaur with five gigantic jaws and two frightening eyes which could roll in all directions. She got up from the floor, looked at her monster, and said softly to herself: "We could make it healthy."

She reached for the baby-bottle. "Put some milk in it." Sucking it, she listlessly walked about the room until she discovered a large cardboard box. "Funny, you always know what I need so badly," she said as she climbed into the box and lay down pulling her knees up to her chin. "And now shut the cover completely. Not a ray of light must come in. It has to be completely dark. And then rock me back and forth, but you have to be completely quiet." I did everything she wished: closed the box, covered it yet with a blanket so that it was totally dark inside, and rocked her slowly to and fro until the end of the hour.

"Just one minute," she begged when that time arrived. She grew very active. In a flash she had drawn a skull on cardboard, mounted it on a long stick, and placed this "flag" in the box, declaring it to be her pirate ship, "Next time I'll play with this."

Then she was ready to leave.

20

"I'll never, ever come and see you again!"

Children who are frequently left home alone, are also intimidated by the repeated warnings of their parents: "Don't let anybody in! Don't play with the matches!" Consider *Struwelpeter*[1] where the mother admonishes her son, "Konrad dear, I'm going out, you'll stay here!" And with raised forefinger proceeds to list the warnings. Where did Betty stand in this respect?

In order to test her I had put a large box of matches on the table, wondering how she would react.

Betty resolutely entered the playroom, objecting right away to the windows being open. "Close the windows! You know I don't like that. People could look in!"

She walked over to the table, turned the candle, and said, "This is the bad side."

"Yes, Betty, it has two sides, a good one and a bad one."

She discovered the matches. "That's fire! Here

[1] Translator's note: The title figure of a sadistic collection of illustrated rhymes about ill-behaved children.

in the box. That's dangerous—the whole house could burn down. Quick, quick, put them away!" Anxiously she pushed the match box toward me.

"You're right, Betty, fire can be dangerous, but if you know how to handle it, fire can also be useful."

"No, no!" she cried out. "My Mommy says fire is very dangerous; the house and everything else can burn down, and then my dress will catch on fire and burn me up and then I'm dead."

"You must be very afraid of fire."

"Put them away, put them away!" she demanded again with a sweeping gesture toward the match box.

"When you hold a burning match in water, it will go out instantly, Betty."

"No, don't light a match. Please, please don't." She looked at me imploringly.

"I won't do it, Betty, unless I have your permission. I assure you nothing will happen. We could first put a pot of water on the table, so the flame will instantly go out in it. You can trust me."

She hesitated a while. (Generally prohibitions are also temptations.) Then she gave her consent.

As agreed, I placed a pot of water on the table, and explained to her how to light a match.

"Well, go ahead and do it, Mrs. Ude." The flame burned, and I dipped it into the water.

Betty followed this procedure with great interest. "Do it again! Do it again!"

Very timidly she then lit a match by herself and extinguished it in the water. She did this again and again until all the matches were gone.

Getting up from the table, she suggested, "Let's dress up now." While she was dressing up as an Indian, I tied a colorful sash around my waist. All at once she changed into a shrew. "You wear only what I tell you!" She tore off my sash. I protested slightly. "Don't you budge!"

After she had completed her Indian outfit, she began dressing me up. With a brusque, unfriendly gesture she wound a long scarf around my hips and declared that I looked dumb.

Then she drew a horrible witch with enormous eyes on the floor. Under the dress she colored yellow flames and said to me, "You are my servant now. Get me the gun!" Repeatedly I had to load the gun for her to shoot at the witch. In a rage she let loose her anger, and again and again it was the eyes she wanted to destroy. As if possessed, Betty was unaware of anything around her. She was completely beside herself.

She took off her Indian dress and threw it at me. "Why don't you wear it?"

I held it up in front of me. "I hardly think it'll fit; maybe as a little skirt, at the most." I smiled a little.

Betty was furious. "Stop laughing so stupidly! Stop that stupid laughing! You only want to make fun of me!" She began to beat on me.

"I see you want to wrestle me," I said, nudging her lightly. Betty burst into hysterical screaming. "You hit me; I'll never, ever come and see you again! I'll tell everybody that you hit me!" She threw herself on the floor and had another tantrum.

I could not help her. In my very first hour with her, she had asked me, "What if you are not Mrs. Ude at all; maybe you're bewitched." I had answered her, "That you must find out for yourself."

I stood silently next to her until she calmed down. This day she wanted to take the baby-bottle home with her.

"Good-bye, Betty."

She left the room without a word.

21

". . . Now all the wicked spirits are flying out through the chimney!"

Betty had come directly from school to her therapy. She rushed into the playroom, threw off her satchel, took off her sweater and trousers, and shouted, "I must wash all my clothes! Everything has to be washed! A boy spit at me!" She was beside herself.

"And your clothes are so dirty now that you have to wash them?"

Betty stood before me, as if turned into a pillar of stone. "I feel so sick, Mrs. Ude, so sick. I've got to wash myself! I have to wash everything. How else can I wash off this sickening slime?" (Feelings of disgust are usually linked to digestive disorders, nausea, and vomiting. It is a complex set of symptoms which has its roots in earliest infancy.)

She ran to the table, propped her elbows on it, and in despair hid her face in her hands. "I must call Lisa! She's got to bring me clean clothes!"

"I don't think your clothes got dirty, Betty. But your disgust is tormenting you." She sat at the table, shuddering frequently, and grumbled about

130

that naughty boy. It took her a long time to calm down.

Betty picked up the match box and asked if we could play with the matches again. "One can't play with fire, Betty, but we can do exactly what we did last time." We placed a pot of water on the table. This time Betty started lighting the matches. Suddenly she remarked, "I'd like to make a real big fire once."

"We can't do that here on the table, Betty. But upstairs there is a fireplace in which we can make a big fire. If you want to, we could go up there." Betty agreed readily and even put her sweater and pants back on.

We stood in front of the fireplace. "Now, what do we need first, Betty?"

"A big bucket of water," she replied.

"That's important, Betty." Next we piled up newspaper and kindling, and Betty lit the fire. She was fascinated by the flickering and crackling. We watched the flames in silence.

Suddenly she drew the outline of her hand on newspaper and placed it in the fire. "Now my hand is burning up." She drew her other hand and burned it, too. "And now the feet." She was, as it were, burning herself up. We watched how the forms she drew went up in flames and slowly turned into charred shreds.

Cleaning and burning have the same purging effect on the unconscious. Here Betty had found another way of freeing herself of inner conflicts.

131

Then she switched to drawing ghosts on the newspaper and put them in the fire. Her eyes grew wide whenever the flames seized hold of a ghost. But her greatest pleasure was when the newspaper, ceasing to glow, would writhe and be sucked upward through the chimney. She continued this ghost-burning until the end of the hour.

When Betty heard Lisa's car arrive, she leaned out of the window and shouted, "Look, Lisa, look! All the wicked spirits are flying out through the chimney!"

22

"You know, today was like Paradise!"

The following hour Betty knew right away what she wanted to do: burn ghosts again. "Come on, let's not lose any time!"

As we were about to leave the playroom, she hesitated in front of me. "Well, Betty?"

"I want you to carry me upstairs!" In no time she had taken off her shoes and lay in my arms. She tried to make an excuse for wanting to be held like a baby. "You know, I only let you carry me because I'm not wearing shoes." I nodded understandingly. On our way upstairs, she said, "I love my Mommy most. And you love me most."

"Yes, Betty."

Again we burned ghosts. Betty was drawing them in all kinds of horrifying shapes on paper. We watched them being devoured by the flames; they writhed and became charred, and then were drawn up through the chimney. Betty felt more and more at ease. She spoke about flying. "Are there big balloons that you can fly over houses and forests in? How wonderful!" She began chirping a little song about a big, colorful balloon which would carry her high above the rooftops. The fire glowed and crackled. Betty exclaimed time and again, "Ah, it's so cozy."

She wanted me to carry her downstairs again at the end of the hour. She said when leaving, "You know, today was like Paradise. And whenever I'm sad, I'll think of today and then I'll be happy again."

23

"Wow, that was a great smearing-session!"

This day Betty appeared relaxed. She pressed a colorful feather in my hand. "Here! I found it. I'm giving it to you."

"Thank you very much, Betty! Where did you find it?"

"In the forest. I went for a hike with my girlfriend and her mother."

"And that's where you found this pretty feather?"

"I'm giving it to you," she repeated with emphasis and sat down in the drawing corner. "You know what I would like to do today? I want to paint with really beautiful colors."

"Go ahead and do whatever you like, Betty."

Using the thickest brushes, she mixed water colors. I noticed that she was mixing only calm, warm colors: orange, ochre, a rich yellow, and brown. With flowing movements she applied these colors in broad parallel bands to the paper. She was pleased with the effect of one color flowing into the other. Gradually brown became more and more predominant. She mixed more browns, lavishly covering one sheet after another with it.

"This is a beautiful color," she commented frequently as she painted. (With compulsive neurotics brown plays a specially important role. Brown is the color of feces. Children who have been toilet-trained at too early an age, find release and relaxation in dabbling with brown paint and messing with mud.)

Then she got out the potty and sat down on it. "Today I have to go peepee."

Afterwards she poured her urine into little paper cups, with obvious pleasure. (Betty was repeating the same game here which, according to her mother, she had taken up as a toddler after she had been completely toilet-trained. At home her mother had spanked her for doing this.)

Then she went back to the drawing corner to continue dabbling with the paints. "I have to tell you something. We have an awful teacher right now. She is really stupid and bitchy." Betty must have been talking about the substitute, since Mrs. Sibilsky has been in the hospital for several days.

"Then, you don't like your new teacher?"

"She scolds the whole time. She's nasty to all the kids."

"You liked Mrs. Sibilsky better?"

"Mrs. Sibilsky is so nice. I hope she gets well soon."

"And how do you like school aside from that?"

"It's okay. I have the nicest girl-friend in my class. Her name is Lilli."

"I'm glad to hear that, Betty."

"She is so nice. I told her about you already. Can I bring her along some time?"

"Certainly, if you'd like to."

"But you must be really kind to her."

"Then, you want me to be just as kind to Lilli as I am to you?"

While I was playing around with some clay, Betty said, "I've got an idea. You knead a real big poopoo and then I'll paint it brown. When we finished, she said, "There, now we'll put it in the potty." After she had done this, she queried: "Now shall I knock over all my paints?"

"You know we have a special room for smearing, where you can do anything you wish." She grabbed the bucket of brown paint and a lump of clay and walked into the next room. With sparkling eyes she first splashed the paint on the wall, then tossed the clay after it. She sprayed the mess with a thick water hose. "Wow, that was a great smearing-session!"

Off she bounced.

Betty, then, had a girl-friend, and she even wanted to bring her to a play session. That was a good step forward, since in the beginning of her therapy she had repeatedly asked me anxiously, "There are so many little children in the city. What if they all wanted to come and visit you?" And she had said, "I don't want you to like the other kids in my class!" I wondered how things would develop, whether Betty in fact would bring her friend, Lilli, and how she would behave in that situation.

24

"Here you can play whatever you like!"

The following time Betty indeed appeared hand in hand with her friend, Lilli. I first greeted Betty, and then told Lilli that I was happy Betty had invited her. Considering Betty's jealousy, it seemed advisable to me to be cautious of my behavior toward Lilli.

Betty turned to Lilli, "Here you can play whatever you like, whatever you really feel like doing."

Lilli, a sturdy, blonde girl, knew immediately what she wanted to do; she wanted to cook. "You are my children, and I'll cook for you."

But Betty had other ideas. She first wanted to show Lilli the far more wonderful things one could do here: make mud-pies—

Lilli refused.

Or burn ghosts in a real, big fire—

"Oh, you and your ghosts! There are no ghosts!" Lilli protested.

"Or we could all go and sit cozily in the bathroom, and Mrs. Ude will tell us a story."

"Why go to the bathroom?" Lilli was surprised. "I don't need to go."

Lilli turned to me, "Why can't I cook, if that's what I feel like doing?"

"The two of you must come to an agreement," I replied discreetly.

Lilli asked Betty, "Are we going to play by ourselves, or will Mrs. Ude play with us?"

Meanwhile Betty had sat down on the swing and pulled on the boxing gloves. She responded brusquely, "Mrs. Ude always plays with us. All three of us'll play together."

"Good," Lilli said, unruffled, and returned to her first suggestion. "I'll be the mother, you be my children, and I'll cook for you."

Betty leaped off the swing, and pretended to box Lilli. Lilli was not upset in the least. "But you have to give me one boxing glove," she demanded. Betty consented, and they engaged in a boxing-wrestling match. Whereas Lilli seemed to freely enjoy this scuffle, it was obvious that Betty was trying to get rid of her aggressions. At times her face had a grim expression. Lilli seemed oblivious, laughing and enjoying the tussle. Wrestling on the floor, Betty at last appeared less tense. Lilli seemed a truly good angel for her.

"What shall we do next?" Lilli asked.

"I know," said Betty, "let's knead puppet heads." Lilli was agreeable to that. We crouched over a large tub of clay and began kneading. While Lilli swiftly created a princess and placed a white veil and crown on her head, Betty formed a ghost-head with hollow eyes.

"You and your ghosts all the time," Lilli grumbled, eyeing her little princess with pride. But she added that you need horror-dolls, too, to put on a puppet show, which I confirmed.

While we continued kneading, Lilli put several insignificant questions to me, which I answered objectively. Suddenly Betty threw her clay head on the floor and started to cry, complaining, "You always talk only to Lilli. You're not nice to me at all today. You're mean to me, because Lilli is here." She curled up in the armchair, pressed her face into the pillows, and sobbed pitifully. She would not listen to Lilli's kind entreaties.

After a while I said to her, "Sometimes Cille is just as sad as you are now. She is sad when you are here because she is afraid that you will crowd her out." Betty still sobbed. I continued, "And now you are just as sad as Cille, because Lilli is here."

Her sobbing ceased. "That's not true, I'm not jealous at all. You're just mean to me." Already her voice had a stubborn ring to it.

Lilli did not let herself be distracted and disappeared to the cooking corner to concoct what she called green wobble-pudding. Betty got herself the baby-bottle, filled it with raspberry juice, and returned, sulking, to her soft armchair.

As the girls said good-bye, Betty turned to Lilli, "I'll never bring you along again."

Lilli said, "I don't want to anyway."

25

"Grow, onion, grow!"

At our next session Betty came with a doll for the first time. I could tell by the way she held it that she was not a good mother to her dolls. She held it carelessly dangling by one leg and let it drop on the table.

Propping her elbows on the table, Betty sighed deeply, "Oh, Mrs. Ude, I always am so happy here with you."

"You look forward to this play hour, just as I always look forward to seeing you, Betty."

She was silent, and waited a while before she spoke again. "Where is Cille?"

"She's taking a walk!"

"Is she still so jealous, the sweety?"

I nodded. "I think so."

"I'll never bring Lilli along anymore so that I won't get so sad again."

"You can decide whether you want to bring her along or not, Betty."

"Why did I have to cry so hard when Lilli was here?"

"Yes, you cried when Lilli was here," I repeated.

She looked directly at me. "I really think I'm very jealous."

"I want to tell you a story, Betty. There once was a little girl who lived together with her Daddy and Mommy for four years. She was the only child of her parents. When she was four years old, a little brother was born. Now she was no longer the only child. Still the parents loved the little girl just as much as before, but they now had to give her brother some of their attention. The grandparents, the aunts and uncles—everybody who came—did not talk only with the little girl, but also with her little brother.

"This made the little girl very sad, because she was afraid that the others no longer loved her as much. And sometimes she even became really angry at her little brother. She was no longer as loving with her dolls—"

Betty had been listening attentively, then she interrupted me. "And that little girl's name is Betty."

"Yes," I repeated, "the girl's name is Betty."

Our eyes met. There was no restlessness, no despair or hate in her eyes. I noticed that her left eyelid wasn't drooping as usual; she seemed more at peace with herself.

My story was intended to help Betty understand herself better. She had admitted, "I really think I'm very jealous." Had I simply confirmed her insight, she would have been left alone at the mercy of her jealousy. A straightforward explanation for the reasons behind her jealousy would merely have resulted in a sterile, intellectual discussion, without furthering the therapeutic process. This simple story, however, let her feel the sorrow of the other girl, she could identify with her and feel herself better understood as well. It is the feeling that counts, not the intellectual comprehension. Only emotional experiences advance the therapeutic process.

While I was absorbed in these thoughts—for maybe a minute—Betty had turned her attention to the flower boxes. "I'd like to plant something." There were onion bulbs ready to be planted. First she looked at them for a long time. "Will they grow if I plant them?"

"All you need to do is to stick them in the soil, and then they'll grow."

"And they'll grow roots?"

"Why don't you try it?"

She went ahead and stuck all the onions into the soil, watered them, and mumbled like a little magician, "Grow, onion, grow." Afterward she washed her hands. I noticed that her washing was no longer a ritual; yet she sniffed at two or three towels before choosing one. She checked her onions again. "Do you really think they'll grow?"

Unexpectedly she went to the sink, filled a bowl alternately with cold and hot water, checking the temperature. She set the bowl on the floor, pulled up a little chair to sit in. Then she took off her shoes and socks, and placed her feet in the bowl. "My feet are dirty, they have to be washed. Will you please wash my feet for me?"

"You would like me to wash your feet, Betty?"

She nodded, splashing the water gently with her feet. I lathered them well.

"More bubbles, much more foam," she demanded. While I was washing her feet, she leaned back, fully relaxed. I told her baby stories which she made me repeat several times. I held her little toe. "This one shakes the plums. This one gathers them up. This one puts them in the basket. This one carries them home . . . and the big one gobbles them all up." She giggled, lolling contentedly.

The hour was over. She put on her socks and shoes and left the playroom smiling.

26

"I want to be a frog!"

Betty had not forgotten the onions. She had hardly stepped into the room, when she demanded, "How are my onions?" She was happy that green shoots had emerged. She looked up at me, "I wonder whether they have roots, too?"

She pulled out an onion. And indeed, the onion had grown tiny roots in just these few days. Betty was delighted. Then she dug out all the onions, and observed with sparkling eyes, "They all have roots."

I assumed she would now stick the onions back into the soil. But what was she doing? She tore out their green shoots and then their roots and removed the outer skin.

"There," she said. "And now I'll wash them, and put them back into the soil." She washed the onions, and loosened the soil with her hands. "I want the onions to have a very soft bed." She buried them deeply in the flower boxes, spreading the soil carefully, and watered them. "Do you think, they'll grow again?"

"You were rather hard on them," I replied, "you

145

tore off their shoots, their roots, and even their skin."

Now she spoke conjuringly to the onions: "You must grow, you must grow and grow; I want you to grow." Like a magician she described circles over the onions with her hands. (A child's fascination with magic is especially pronounced once he has reached that stage of his development where he begins to feel guilt. At this stage the Oedipal complex gradually passes while the first traces of the super-ego develop. This takes place between the age of four-and-a-half and seven. With magic, the child tries to get the world into his grasp and experiences a strengthening of his ego.)

Then she ran to the swing and began soaring high up to the ceiling, singing: "I'm flying, I'm flying high into the sky, into the sky, into the sky."

After that she wanted something to drink and poured juice in the baby-bottle. She pushed the nipple aside. "I don't need it anymore, I'm a big girl now. And I can do gymnastics, too. Look!"

She performed various stunts for me, did a handstand, turned cartwheels and somersaults. She was very agile.

Then she told me that she had been invited to a friend's birthday party. Each child was to come dressed up as something. "Ah," I was curious, "and what will you be?"

"A witch," she blurted out. "Hee, hee, hee, will I ever scare them! I'll fly in on a broom."

"I'd like to see what such a witch looks like," I said.

Immediately Betty picked up the colored pencils to draw a picture for me. She snickered like a little witch, as she drew a broom (picture 22).

I was impressed and delighted with her picture. "Those two will surely have a lot of fun at the party. They look so jolly!"

Suddenly Betty became very angry. She tore the paper from my hand, yelling, "You're stupid, really stupid! You just try to annoy me all the time—with your stupid laughing."

She ran to a corner and threw a ball back at me. "You think I'm a witch! You don't love me." She marched up to me and demanded desperately, "Now tell me that you love me!" Again there was that expression of despair and loneliness on her face.

"You are afraid, Betty, that I no longer love you as a witch. But how often have I told you"—She interrupted me and without taunting finished my speech:

"That you always love me, . . . whether I'm good or bad, pretty or ugly." She smiled a little.

"That's right, Betty." How quickly she recovered now!

She pointed to Peter's candle with its two sides. "Maybe Peter was bewitched sometimes, too, and that's why he made this candle. Maybe he freed himself from the evil spell with it."

We then sat on the floor together and played

with the clay. I deliberately formed a large heart to see how Betty would respond to it. The heart is the symbol of feeling. Betty looked at the heart. Without a word she crushed it with her feet.

I deplored this, saying: "I don't think that's nice at all. A heart is so important."

"Oh, shut up!" she snapped. "Spiders[1] are more important to me. Let's play puppet theater. Play a story for me, but you have to make it up yourself."

From behind the stage, I then put on an improvised fairy-tale. A frog appeared, and mournfully told the audience that it once had been a princess, but had been changed into a frog because of its cold heart. Now the frog wanted to have a warm heart and turn back into a princess. She was tired of living in the water. An old woman came along, and the frog poured out its troubles. She told the frog that it must dive deep down into the water without fearing the monsters in the depths. It would come to a meadow on the bottom of the sea, where colorful flowers bloomed. The frog should be on the lookout for an especially beautiful flower which it should press against its heart. The frog would then feel itself grow warmer and warmer, and then it would be transformed back into a princess with a heart. The frog did as the old woman had bade, and came back to earth as a happy princess.

She found her prince, and after celebrating a wonderful wedding, they lived happily ever after.

Betty had paid close attention to the performance.

[1] See also page 26.

148

At the end she decided emphatically, "I want to be a frog!" (Betty still wanted to be a frog, a cold-blooded being with a cold heart.)

She ran to the blackboard and drew a big green frog on it. "That's what I want to be, a frog, a big, green frog. And I don't want you to erase it before next time."

"Okay, fine!"

She ran off in good spirits.

27

"If Lisa gets married, Sebastian and I will be all alone!"

It was another Tuesday. Betty arrived, waving a sheet of drawing paper in her hand (picture 23). "Here, for you. Lisa told me to give this to you."

My reaction to it was apparently of no interest to her.

Two things stand out clearly in this picture: the heart and the word "Arzt" (doctor). Should a doctor come, because the heart is sick? Was it a reaction to the previous hour where she had crushed the heart and wanted to remain a frog?

Betty ran directly to her onions. She observed joyfully that they showed green shoots again. "And also little roots." As before, she pulled all the onions from the soil, twisted off their green shoots and roots, peeled and washed them, and stuck them back in the soil. She looked at me. "Do you think, they'll grow again?" I hesitated. "I think so."

Betty insisted, "Even if everyone thinks that they won't grow, they will grow; they must grow, they are very strong!" She obviously wished to identify with the strength of the onions.

Then she jumped with her feet on the swing.

"Now, watch out," she called, "I'm going to let myself fall into your arms. You catch me! And hold me! And carry me!" she exclaimed during this game. "Now I am falling from the sky to the earth."

Afterward she pumped the swing vigorously and was overjoyed every time she touched the ceiling with her toes. As she did this she wanted me to say the same sentence over and over: "Into the sky, into the sky." She grew freer and freer, and laughed heartily.

Then as the swing slowly stopped, she looked serious. "You know," she said, "yesterday I was really sad and cried. When I have to cry again, I'll simply think of this laughing, and then everything will be well again."

"You cried?"

"Yes," she said, "I was out with my friend Lilli and her mother, and I suddenly had the feeling of not having a mother at all. My Mommy is on a trip again. If Lisa gets married some day, then Sebastian and I will be all alone."

"Even if one isn't all alone," I said, "one sometimes feels that way. I can understand that."

For a moment Betty gave in to her sadness. Then she said that what she would enjoy most was playing hide-and-seek. "You have to look for me. Go quickly behind the door, and don't come back in until I say it's okay."

When I came back into the room, I discovered her immediately. She had crawled under a shelf with the tips of her feet sticking out. Still, I walked back and forth around the room, and searched for her everywhere. "Where could she be? Not here. Not there. Why, how could she just disappear?" My search went on and on. "Betty, Betty! where on earth is she? I'm truly starting to get worried."

There was a soft giggle, and then to her immense joy she was found. She wanted to repeat this game over and over. She wanted me to search and find her every time, making such comments as, "You get really scared, don't you, when you can't find me?" and, "You go on looking for me, until you finally find me." She was at ease after this game. Obviously it helped her overcome her fear of being abandoned.

When she said good-bye that day, she shook my hand for the first time.

"You're kind, Mrs. Ude. See you on Friday!"

28

"When I grow up to be a mother, I can't have a boy, because then I'd make a bad mother!"

The next Tuesday Betty came skipping into the room. "Look here what I can do." She turned a cartwheel and several somersaults. "I'm the best in gym class."

She rushed to her onions and clapped her hands with joy, "They're green again!" She tore one onion from the soil, "And it has roots, too." She stuck it back into the soil at once "Now I'll leave them in their bed where they feel strong and content." She looked up at me, "You see, they grew like mad, because I peeled them down completely. You didn't think they would, did you? And now we're both happy that they did grow after all."

"Yes, Betty, we're both very happy about that."

She ran over to the table to grab a handful of candy and for the first time shared one with me.

"Oh, thank you very much, Betty." Silently we sat together, sucking our candies.

Then Betty asked, "Will you have a baby some time soon?"

"No, Betty. Why do you ask?"

"When I'm as big as you are, I want to be a mother."

"Oh, so you'd like to have children when you're grown up?"

"Yes, but only a girl, not a boy."

"You want to be a mother one day, but you don't want to have a boy?"

"When I grow up to be a mother, I can't have a boy, because then I'd make a bad mother."

"You must be afraid, then, that a bad sister could one day become a bad stepmother," I confronted her, perhaps too daringly.

She looked at me with surprise and answered hesitantly, "Maybe it will wash away one day—my jealousy—but Cille is even more jealous than I am—that sweeeet Cille." Whenever she spoke of Cille her voice became soft and sentimental. She adored my little dog.

"But, after all, Cille is a dog, Betty, and you are a person." She didn't want to talk about this any more, but sat down in front of the puppet theater instead. "Tell me a story, but only one you made up!"

The tale of the little brother and his sister seemed to me most fitting at the moment. I even had a large colored picture which showed a little girl embracing a fawn. Without saying a word, I placed this picture in front of the stage. "Is that going to be the story?" Betty asked.

"Yes," I returned, "I now will tell you the tale of Little Brother and Little Sister.

"Once upon a time there was a little brother

154

and a little sister, and they had a bad stepmother. She scolded the children all the time and gave them only bread crusts to eat. One day when she was especially mean to the children, Little Brother and Little Sister took each other's hand and said, 'Let's go far away together into the big world. It can't be any worse than it is here!' "

As the story progressed, Betty soon became totally wrapped up in the ventures of Little Brother and Little Sister. She called to them, telling them where they could find the best place to sleep, and warning them of dangers.

When Little Brother then got thirsty and wanted to drink from the well that the witch-stepmother had cast a spell on, Betty increased her anxious calls and warnings to Little Brother. Still, he drank and was changed into a fawn. Betty was now totally absorbed in the little sister's devoted care for her fawn-brother.

I shortened the story. The sister married a prince who was very powerful in his kingdom. His men searched for the witch, found her and burned her at the stake.

Thereupon the fawn-brother was freed from the spell and turned into a human being again.

Betty was so moved by this story that she knelt down before the large picture of Little Brother and Little Sister and kissed the fawn. "Now all is well again, Little Brother. Now the bad stepmother is dead; now nothing can happen to you anymore; now you are a real person again."

She wanted to sketch the bad witch once more

on the floor. With astonishing speed she drew a frightening life sized witch with long, thin fingers and big green eyes to which she added slits instead of round pupils, since they were supposed to be "evil cat eyes." She drew ugly rags over her as clothes with flames blazing under her.

Then she got herself a little pail of mud. She stood before the witch. "And now you must die, because you were so evil to Little Brother and Little Sister." She hurled lumps of mud at the evil eyes, exclaiming with satisfaction, "There! There!" Finally she stomped around on the bemired witch.

As she left the room at the end of the hour, she said calmly, "This was the most beautiful hour of all."

29

"I have to sleep and sleep and sleep"

Next time Betty arrived carrying a large bundle under her arm. "I brought my bed today," she said. It was wrapped together with her favorite animals in a large plastic bag. With these treasures she curled up in the big, soft armchair. Again her face twitched and her left eyelid drooped, a symptom which the eye doctor had diagnosed as a sign of extreme exhaustion. "Today I don't want to do anything," she said tiredly, "I don't feel like swinging or eating candy; I have to sleep and sleep and sleep." From her little purse she produced a pair of scissors and a string. She then cut holes in the plastic bag and pulled the string through them. It was some time before she explained what she intended with this. Pointing to the plastic bag, she said, "I'm going to pull this over my head now. No rain, no cold can come in. I'm completely protected under here, and I want to stay under here forever. This is my bed. Nobody may touch it, except my Mommy and you."

Another deep regression, after nearly a year of therapy, I thought, watching her. She cowered under her little blanket with the plastic bag pulled over her. Her eyes were closed. Around her wrist she was wearing a little bracelet to which she had attached a home-made skeleton. She remained burrowed in like that for quite a while. As she pushed the plastic cover aside, she pressed her hand to her forehead, saying, "The worst thing is when I have a headache, and this sick feeling. It's here in my head. I can't think. I must be stupid. Today I did math with my Mommy and I couldn't think. I did very poorly. I must be dumb."

"There are such times, Betty, when it's hard to think right, when you're exhausted. But that doesn't last and it does not mean that you're dumb."

"But you, you're never sick?" She looked at me dejectedly.

"Oh yes, that happens to me, too, and then I can't think right either."

Then she pushed the plastic cover away completely and sat up in the armchair. She was wearing her hair in braids that day for the first time. "You haven't said anything about my new hair-style yet!" And she immediately added, "My Mommy doesn't like it." She looked at me full of expectation. A compliment seemed important to her.

"You know, sometimes Cille's long ears look just like braids." I needed to say no more. The comparison with Cille sufficed to make her feel accepted. She laughed a little and exclaimed, "I've got ear-braids! Just like Cille—that sweet, little Cille."

She ambled around the room. Nothing felt right to her—everything was "dumb"; the candies, my clothes, the toys.

"Let's mess around with the clay," she suggested finally. As we were sitting on the floor, each of us kneading some clay in his own way, she continued to let out her aggressions. "I bet you'd love to stir around in pee." She looked at me in defiance. "I'll change you into an old hag and flush you down the toilet." Next she took a clump of clay. After hurling it onto the floor several times, she began to form things out of it: first plain balls, then a heart. She broke off lollipop sticks and speared them into the heart. Then she formed two more hearts. On one she painted a large eye and on the other three violet crosses. (Here she expressed the same problem as in picture 23: her heart was sick, her feelings were still crucified, a doctor was needed. Violet is the color of mysticism, of mourning.) Then she took everything she had formed into both hands and, with a mixed expression of delight and despair, squeezed it hard. She sat listlessly on the floor. After awhile she got up and climbed with her feet on the board of the swing. "Catch me!" She let herself fall backwards into my arms over and over again.

A few minutes before the end of her hour she curled up in the armchair again. "Tell me a story, please!"

I tried to encourage her to act out a fairy-tale on her own, since this would more readily help her bring out and resolve unconscious conflicts. She refused, insisting rather that I tell her a fairy-tale. "But you have to make it up."

Before starting, I quickly considered the events

of this hour: with the plastic cover she had wanted to protect herself from the outside world. She was still too weak to cope with her environment. In my talks with her mother I had repeatedly stressed that Betty's mental blocks in arithmetic were due to psychic conflicts and that all outside pressure only opposed the resolution of these problems. Yet the mother apparently could not cease putting pressure on Betty, with the result: "I'm dumb. I can't think." Also her disapproval of Betty's braids had again given Betty the feeling of being rejected by her mother.

Since Betty was at that time in the phase of fascination with magic, I told her a story of a little girl who, because of her bad stepmother, ran into the forest to tell her woe to the animals. There a good fairy gave her a magic ring which from now on would protect her from all evil.

"Just like Peter's candle!" Betty exclaimed, running to the table, and turned it so that the flower side showed. "Does Peter still need the candle?" she asked suddenly.

"No, he is so strong now that he no longer needs it, Betty."

The hour was over. With a handful of candy and her "bed" under her arm, she took off in good spirits.

30

"Remember how I used to be afraid of open windows, that somebody might come in. Now I'm not afraid anymore."

Betty was a few minutes late. I waited in the playroom, rereading the notes of previous hours. The last hour had brought another severe relapse. In spite of frequent talks with the mother, the same kind of relapses recurred even after thirteen months of therapy.

Betty was in the second grade. She was an average student in all subjects except math, in which she was still deficient at times. She no longer was the "mute" girl. I had continually warned the mother not to drill and put pressure on Betty and tried to call her attention to that which was most important at this time: to protect Betty from a threatening severe neurosis. At times it was difficult for me not to forget that I had to be just as patient with the parents as I was with the child.

Then here came Betty. She was playing on a recorder. "My Mommy bought it for me." Her eyes gleamed as she started to play on it for me, "Row, row, row your boat." It did not sound quite right yet, but she seemed to enjoy it immensely. Again and again she tried to find the right notes, to play the tune as correctly as possible. Her endurance surprised me. Finally she put the recorder aside.

That day I had placed a toy soldering kit on the table. In the previous hours Betty at times had expressed a desire to practice magic and had wanted to be a witch. A witch has magic strength and power. Betty was interested in the kit. After I had explained to her the things one could do with it, she announced, "I'll make a magic ring for myself." She attended to the necessary preparations, bustling about like a little sorceress in her witch's kitchen. But she did not succeed in casting a closed ring.

"That's all right," she decided, and closed the missing third of the ring with clay.

Ceremoniously she pushed the ring onto her finger. "Now I can practice magic. Now I'm strong. Everything has to obey me." She drew three large circles on the floor. "These are my houses. Only I live here—nobody can enter."

Conjuring, she stepped from one circle into the other. "And when I leave my houses," she raised her ringed hand, "nobody can touch me either, because I have a magic ring."

Every time I came close to her, she raised her hand, and I had to step back. She wanted to put her magic strength to a bigger test. "Now you have to do everything, absolutely everything I say." She rubbed her magic ring.

"Go stand in the corner at once!" I did so.

"Lie down on the couch!" I did so.

"Sit on the chair!" I did so.

"Kneel down!" I did so.

"Open the window!" I did so.

For the first time she wanted the windows to be opened. Then we sat down together in the broad windowsill. As the sun shone on her face, she squinted, and I could tell that she was pleased with life today. No nervous twitching; her eyes were clear and centered. A man walked by on the street. "Remember how I used to be afraid of open windows? Afraid that somebody might come in? Now I'm not afraid anymore."

"You are not afraid of strangers anymore, Betty, not even in the city?"

She reflected. "There, maybe a little bit. But only sometimes, and also in the elevator only sometimes. But let's not talk about that. Let's play. What are we going to play?"

"Well, that's up to you to decide, Betty."

"I don't know what. You say what."

"We could play 'I see something you don't see.'[1] And only those things count which we see outside the window."

With this game I wanted to call Betty's attention wholly to the street, to people and objects which were strange to her, which she had always feared so much. She agreed readily to the game. Before we started, Betty quickly hopped to the table to get a bag of candy which she placed between us.

[1] In this children's game one person must guess at an object which the other person has described only by its color.

"Let's munch a little in between; that makes it so cozy."

I was to start. "I see something you don't see, and that is—black."

Betty enjoyed the game. She guessed at everything, naming all the black objects she saw in the street. At last she discovered the black hat which a man, sitting on a bench across the street, was wearing. With this guessing game the hour passed in no time. As Betty was leaving, she told me: "I'm looking forward to next time."

"So am I, Betty."

From now on the gaps in my account of Betty's therapy will be wider than before, since the sessions with Betty were increasingly repetitive, and regressions to earlier stages of development rarely occurred.

31

"My house!"

This day Betty came storming into the playroom.
"Let's not lose any time, hurry!" She pulled me
to the windowsill to begin once again our guessing
game. She opened the window and then fetched
candy and little bottles of soy sauce from the toy
storecounter. She gave orders, "You get a pillow
for each of us, so we'll be real comfortable." We
sat on the windowsill again and played "I see
something you don't see." Betty munched her candy,
offering me some, too. As we nipped at our bottles
of soy sauce, she said, "I'm so glad that you like
soy sauce, too; that makes it really cozy."

Our guessing game lasted quite a while. When
Betty left the windowsill, she headed resolutely
for the cardboard box standing in the far corner,
the same box in which she had wanted me to rock
her like a baby many months before.

What was she up to this time?

She dragged it into the middle of the room, while
I looked on idly. She criticized, "You could give
me a hand, you know."

"But I don't know what you're going to do with
it, Betty."

"You'll see in a minute," she returned perkily,

setting the large box on its side so that its flaps resembled large doors. With colored pencils she drew windows with curtains on the outside walls and sketched knobs on the doors.

"Aha!" I exclaimed, "It is going to be a house."

"My house," she retorted and went on working.

She crawled into her house, placed a mat on its floor, and decorated the inside walls with framed flower pictures. She bustled about eagerly. Next she pushed a stick through the "roof," explaining, "That's the chimney."

Then I had to gather all the candy and soy sauce bottles, and crowd into her house with her. When I mentioned that I would prefer if one could open the windows, she dismissed my suggestion. "After all, not just anybody can look into my house; it's enough that the doors can be opened." I agreed with her, but added that I still would like it better if one could open the windows at least sometimes, to have a better view and to let in more fresh air and sunlight.

"Oh, well, it's bright enough for me. After all, the doors are so large. Come and help me build a garden around the house."

We dragged the flower boxes in front of the house. Betty dug her little fingers into the soil. "It's time we get beautiful flowers in here."

She mounted colored paper on straws. I, too, had to make my share of flowers. Soon she had a colorful flower garden in front of her house. We placed the little bench in the garden and sat down to rest on it.

167

Betty was obviously satisfied with her house and garden. She started to chat. "Ah, if only my little Munchy were here now, how nicely he could run around in this garden."

"Your Munchy?"

"Yes, that's right. I didn't tell you yet that I have a little bunny. My Mommy bought it for me yesterday."

"You have a little bunny?"

Betty went on, "Yes, yes, a bunny. Actually, I wanted a dog, but my Mommy thought that a dog wouldn't feel comfortable in an apartment. He needs a garden to dig in. But now I'm happy about my bunny; it lives in my room and belongs only to me all by myself. I'm its mother, just like you're the mother of Cille."

"Yes," I said, "now we each have a pet and must take care of it like mothers. We must never forget them." I listed everything that had to be done for an animal to keep it healthy. "One must feed it, give it water or milk, keep it clean, and pet it often so that it won't feel so alone."

Betty nodded approvingly. "I'll do all that for my Munchy."

"And a bunny is an entirely different animal, Betty, from a dog or a bird or a fish; and of course it is also different from a person. A bunny doesn't want to eat candy or bones which dogs like so much. You should find out what a bunny needs to eat."

"I know that already," Betty said with some satisfaction. "Carrots, fresh grass, and things like

168

that: that's what it likes."

"And it also needs sun sometimes."

"Yes, I know. Every time I go to my Grandma, I'll take Munchy with me and let him play in her large meadow.

"Well, then I'm sure Munchy is in good hands with you, Betty."

She brought out a sketch-pad to draw Munchy. She wasn't satisfied with any of her drawings and crossed out every one. "Munchy is much, much more beautiful; I can't draw him that beautiful. I better bring him along for you to see some time."

"I'll look forward to him, and I'll have fresh carrots ready for him."

"But don't forget!"

"Definitely not!"

The clock announced the end of the hour. With satisfaction, Betty took a final glance at her beautiful house. "Leave everything the way it is, so that next time we can play with it right away."

"You'll find it untouched. Good-bye. Say hello to Munchy for me!"

"And you say hello to Cille from me, the little jealous girl! Good-byyyye!" she called playfully and ran off.

After Betty had left the room, I remained sitting on the bench for a moment. "Good, old cardboard box," I thought. "You have come a long way with us. First you were a cradle—maybe even the womb which Betty wanted to go back to. You had to be completely dark and quiet inside, and all she wanted was to be cradled gently back and forth in you. Then you were turned into a pirate ship with a death-banner. And today you are a house, her house, her first house with an open door!" (The house is a symbol for the self. See page 34.) The inside was decorated with pictures of flowers, and a soft rug was on the floor. A house with a chimney to let out the smoke. The windows were only a facade, yet one could already feel at home in this house. And in front of the house was a garden with flowers, which Munchy would have liked.

I couldn't help but think of my second session with Betty, where she said, "There are rats. They live underground, they grub and gnaw. Sometimes they are in the attic, too, or in the cellar."

32

"Now I have all the ghosts firmly in my hand!"

From the door I watched Betty arrive with her mother. They hugged and kissed each other good-bye, and Betty ran happily up to me. She danced in circles, swinging her skirt high: "Isn't this a pretty dress?"

She then told me how she had ridden on the bus that day all by herself to see her friend Felix who had a Siamese cat. And yesterday she had gone to the circus with her Mommy and two girl-friends. She was thrilled with this visit and told about the animals and the clowns, which she had enjoyed so much.

She wandered through the room until she stopped in front of her house. "Ah, my beautiful house. You left everything just as I wanted it. That was nice of you."

She sat down on the swing and pushed herself way up to the ceiling. As she slowly let the swing come to a halt, she asked, "And what shall we do today?"

Well, Betty, what do *you* want to do today?"

"I know. You close your eyes and I'll build something. But don't peek."

"I promise, Betty."

After a while she called me. She had built a cave in which I was to visit her. I was shocked. Sketches of large ghosts and monsters were scattered all around. She explained, "These ghosts are very, very evil and dangerous, but you don't have to be afraid when I'm here; they can't hurt you. Now I have all the ghosts firmly in my hand!"

She jumped out of her cave, tore up all the ghosts and monsters, and said, "Let's not talk about them anymore, let's not even draw them anymore, either! Remember how we used to do that? Remember when we let them fly out through the chimney? Remember? Remember?" With remarkable accuracy Betty then recounted all the hours in which she had destroyed ghosts. Her memory was astounding.

Afterward she went to the xylophone. Sounding the notes with the hammers, she moved from the lowest to the highest and back down to the lowest notes, accompanying their sound with melodious phrases.

"Up here is heaven and down here is hell; up here is peace and down here is death; up here is goodness and down here is evil. Here one can play everything; here one can always be the way one happens to be."

Then she sat down on the floor with a piece of chalk. She drew a very big heart and asked me, "Would you make me a big heart like this and give it to me as a present?"

With clay I filled in the large heart she had

drawn, slid a piece of cardboard under it so that it would not fall apart, and presented it to her.

She was overjoyed. Then she said, "We could write a name on it."

"Or just a letter?" I asked cautiously, "Maybe a B, Betty?"

"No, no!" she objected, "not a B."

Pondering, she at last decided, "C. U. and M. U.; Cille Ude and Munchy Ude."

I looked at her. "Are you sure?"

She corrected, "No, just a big C and a big M; Cille and Munchy."

Then Betty formed hearts with clay. She made big and little ones, decorating many of them with colorful candies or marzipan and chocolate chips.

She considered taking a heart along for Sebastian, but eventually forgot about it.

An important hour was over; Betty had discovered the "heart."

33

"The hearts have to be very sweet!"

This day Betty did not come alone. She was carrying her little rabbit, Munchy, under her arm. Munchy must have had good handling, because he was not in the least nervous. His name suited him well; his muzzle was continuously moving, although he was not eating. Betty never forgot anything. "Weren't you going to give him nice, fresh carrots to eat?"

"Oh, yes, I completely forgot. I have no carrots in the house."

"But you said yourself that one should never forget the animals."

"That's right, Betty, but you didn't tell me that you were going to bring Munchy today. I thought you might bring him last time." She looked at me searchingly.

"Did you have carrots last time?" She saw right through me.

"To be honest, no, I didn't. I forgot the carrots last time, too."

She hung down her head. "I'm sad that you forgot." She was crushed.

"I know, Betty; because to forget means that

one has left someone alone, has forgotten him. And when you feel left alone, you get sad, disappointed, and even afraid. And everything that happens to Munchy happens to you as well, because you love him so much."

She looked up at me. "When I have to wait a long time for my Mommy, I get afraid, because I think that she has forgotten me and will never come back."

"And right now you felt the same sadness, Betty. You were afraid that I was forgetting you and Munchy and that is why you were so sad."

"But now I'm not sad anymore," she said cheerfully and sat down on the floor to take up the same work as last time, forming hearts with clay. After she had completed a whole series of hearts, she went to get a bag of sugar.

"The hearts have to be very sweet." She sprinkled sugar over them.

At the end of the hour she considered her brother again. "Today I'll take a really beautiful heart along for Sebastian." And she wrapped the heart in colored paper, tied a ribbon around it. But then forgot it after all.

34

"Oh Mommy, I love you so much!"

Since her first session Betty had not built anything with the Sceno-box. After eighteen months of therapy a second test happened almost naturally. The Sceno-box always stood in the playroom, had always been ready for use, yet it had never interested her. Today I had placed it on the table where I always kept the sweets, so that Betty could not fail to see it.

"Look at the things I can do," Betty exclaimed as she skipped into the room. She did a handstand, turned cartwheels and somersaults, jumped with her feet onto the board of the swing and while swinging turned a somersault.

"My goodness!" I exclaimed. "You're a real acrobat, Betty!" Full of pride and joy she performed more stunts for me and mentioned, as once before, that she was in fact the best in her gym class: on the trampoline she could jump high enough to touch the ceiling with her fingertips. It was a delight to watch her. How beautifully she was built. Her movements were both vigorous and graceful. With her sparkling eyes and ruddy cheeks she looked like a little princess right out of a fairy-tale.

"Bravo, bravo," I applauded time and again. At last she was totally out of breath and let herself drop onto a bench. She discovered the opened Sceno-box.

"The first time I was here, I built something with these things. Remember? You said to me, 'If you like, you can build something with these things,' and I did."

"If you like, you can do it again today," I retorted, marveling at her excellent memory.

Right away she set to work, building a spacious apartment. First she set up her playroom, arranging it exactly like her room at home. Munchy was there, too. Next came the kitchen. In front of the stove she placed a young woman and said, "This is Lisa, she bakes and cooks for the family." Then she furnished the living-room and placed a woman in an armchair. "That's Mommy. She's reading a book." On the rocking-horse she put a little boy. "That's Sebastian." A male figure was sitting at a table. "That's Daddy."

Now her story began: a girl came running into the room, sat down on Daddy's lap, and cuddled up to him. Then she ran up to the mother, hugged her, and said, "Oh Mommy, I love you so much!" Betty took the little boy off the rocking-horse and put him on a rug with a few toys. "Thank you for the rocking-horse, Sebastian." She carried it into her playroom.

Then she had the little girl announce, "Today

we'll celebrate my birthday." All her friends arrived. Lilli, her best friend, brought her a little bear as a present. Then Betty remembered that she wanted to have a large garden in front of the house, with a lawn, trees, and flowers, and a big swimming-pool. When that was arranged, they went on celebrating in the garden. Grandma and Grandpa arrived too. Grandma slipped and fell into the pool. Mommy and Lisa rescued her from the water and laid her on a deck-chair. Grandma was unconscious. "It serves her right for not paying attention." Betty remarked. "And now you've got your punishment for being so mean to me yesterday." After a while Grandma recovered. They celebrated late into the evening. Her friends said good-bye, adding, "That was a beautiful birthday party, Betty." And so Betty's Sceno-play ended.

"I love this game," Betty remarked. "Next time I'll play with it again." She ran to the reception room to see whether Lisa had arrived yet. Lisa was already waiting. Hurriedly Betty said good-bye. "When I come home, my Mommy and Daddy will be back from their trip. I can't wait to see them! Byyyye, Mrs. Ude!"

"Good-bye, Betty!"

I reread my notes on Betty's first Sceno-test. At that time she had placed a baby under a Christmas tree, circling a gander and fox around it, saying, "Here comes the bad fox sneaking up." With this she had conveyed her unconscious aggression toward her little brother. Then the crocodile had attacked the cow. "Huuugh, this is getting dangerous now," she had commented, demonstrating her unconscious struggle with her mother. And to my question, "Where are you in this game?" she had answered, "I'm not there."

In her second Sceno-play she had made herself the center of attraction by celebrating her birthday with her friends and family. Life was full of joy for her now. The mother-daughter and brother-sister relationship in this Sceno indicated a positive change. The anal complex, which was brought out in the first Sceno-test, was altogether missing in this second test. The incident where she simply let the grandmother slip into the water, she tried to take out her annoyance with her grandmother about something that had happened the previous day.

The Sceno-game is not only an excellent diagnostic, but a valuable therapeutic aid as well.

A Call from Betty

The telephone rang. It was Betty.

"Yes, Betty?"

"I'd like so much to go ice-skating with my friend Lilli. Do you mind if I don't come to see you today?"

"Why no, Betty! I'm glad when you can have a nice time with Lilli. You already know how to ice-skate?"

"No, today is my first time, but I'll learn real fast! My Mommy is going with us, you know. I'm looking forward to it sooooo much. Good-bye, Mrs. Ude!"

"Goody-bye, Betty!"

35

"Now the mermaid has to do what the owl told her to do, otherwise she can't turn into a real person."

As soon as Betty arrived, she dragged the rocking-horse in front of the puppet theater, sat down on it and decided, "Let's have a story hour today, and you'll make up a story." The large picture of Little Brother and Little Sister was still leaning against the stage. "Ah!" Betty exclaimed. "How I love this picture of Little Brother and Little Sister, especially the little girl in it. I wish I had a little sister, but if I had a little sister, I probably would want a little brother."

As she said this, our eyes met. I smiled a little, and then she did, too, and claimed, "You know, I'm really not jealous anymore. I sometimes just pretend."

Then I went behind the puppet stage while Betty sat expectantly on the rocking-horse in front of it.

"What are you waiting for, Mrs. Ude?"

I groaned a little. "I don't know, I can't quite think of anything today."

"Just start!"

And then Betty began to tell about the kind

181

of story she wanted to hear. "About a mermaid who is in the water. You know the story, and who wants to be a real person."

I introduced the mermaid sitting on a tree stump and singing a mournful song, " 'Only one hour, a single hour may I stay here on land, but then I must return to the cold, cold water! Woe, woe is me.'

"High up in a tree an owl, who with her golden eyes can see in the dark, heard the mermaid's song. 'I can help you, my dear mermaid,' the owl called, 'but only if you do everything I tell you.' 'I'll do everything, dear owl, everything you say,' the mermaid promised. The owl plucked a feather from her plumage, handed it to the mermaid, and said, 'Take this feather and dive down into the water just once more, but you must dive deep down to the bottom. There you will see a big crocodile with a gaping jaw. Don't be afraid . . . When you touch the crocodile with this feather, you will see that he can't harm you.

" 'Next you will see a long snake. Touch it with the feather as you did the crocodile, and you will see that it, too, can't harm you.

" 'Last you will come upon a big spider. Don't be afraid, but do the same as with the crocodile and the snake, and you will see that it, too, can't harm you.

" 'Finally you will hear a loud thunder, and the waters will hurl you onto the land as a real woman.' "

182

At this point I paused to rest.

"Go on!" Betty called.

I hesitated, "And what do you think should happen next?"

"Well," Betty stated somewhat impatiently, "now the mermaid has to do what the owl told her to do, otherwise she can't turn into a real person." I played everything through in the desired sequence. In the end the mermaid was thrown onto the land as a real woman.

"And her name shall be Lizzi," Betty decided immediately, "and next time you'll tell me how she finds her prince."

"Fine," I said, "to be continued in the next hour. We still have much time. What shall we play now?"

"Maybe something with dice," Betty suggested.

"Are you maybe thinking of Parcheesi?"

"Oh, yes, let's play that."

I briefly explained to her, "In this game you try to get all your men into the goal as fast as possible."

Betty comprehended everything quickly and started to throw the dice. Early in the game she began to cheat, whereas I was playing honestly. I let this pass a while before I said, "But we must agree whether we want to play with or without cheating." She looked at me slightly dumfounded. I explained: "For every game there are rules which one must follow. We have to decide whether we want to play honestly or whether both of us may cheat or whether only you may cheat and I must play honestly." The matter made her uncomfortable, but she realized that a decision had to be made.

"Okay," she declared, "I'm smaller; I may cheat a little now and then. You're grown-up and have to play honestly."

"Good, now we have our rules." Of course Betty won every game. This pleased her immensely. Losing would still have been too hard for her. At the end of the hour she went to the blackboard and wrote, "Betty always won. Mrs. Ude always lost."

She left the playroom a happy winner.

36

"Is the hour over soon?"

Betty arrived with ice-skates flung over her shoulder. "Right after this I'm going skating with Lisa and Lilli. I'm looking forward to it soooo much! I wish the hour were over already."

She put down her skates and sat down at the large table. I admired her little skirt and remarked that ice-skating must be a fine sport. Betty beamed and showed me how one moves on the ice: arms extended at the sides, alternately lifting the left and right leg. "You know, Mrs. Ude, it goes all by itself, you just glide over the ice and don't have to do a thing." She chatted for a good while about the joys of ice–skating. Then she went behind the puppet stage. "Today I will play a story for you. You sit on the rocking-horse and listen. This is Lizzi—the Lizzi who was a mermaid before. Lizzi runs into the forest now and thanks the owl for having helped her so much. A prince comes riding through the forest on his horse. He sees Lizzi. They fall in love with each other. And now they celebrate a big wedding. All the animals are invited, and the owl sits next to Lizzi at the wedding banquet. End!

"You know, Mrs. Ude, my stories are much shorter than yours. I can't stretch the stories out as beautifully as you do."

"But I liked your story very much, Betty."

"What else can we play?" Betty asked. "Is the hour over soon?"

"We still have fifteen minutes." She swung gently to and fro on the swing. "You need a lot of time now for school," I said, "for your friends, for ice-skating, for playing your recorder, for your bunny and for so many other wonderful things. Maybe it would be enough if you only came once a week?"

It was an easy decision for Betty. She nodded contentedly, adding, "And we can always call each other on the phone if we want to."

"Why, certainly, Betty. We can always do that."

Full of anticipation she threw her skates over her shoulder and for the first time said good-bye early. Since Lisa had also arrived early, Betty was able to take off without further delay to enjoy her ice-skating.

37

"Right after this we're going ice-skating together."

The following Friday Betty and her friend Lilli stood in the doorway with their skates over their shoulders. "Right after this we're going ice-skating together. I can't wait! Come on, Lilli, let's swing!" Betty exclaimed happily and stood with her feet on the board while Lilli sat down on it. The two girls swung to and fro, singing a song, a hit song about love. In between they giggled and talked about which teachers and classmates were dumb or nice. It looked as if they were perfectly content by themselves. I withdrew to a far corner of the playroom.

Lilli wanted to cook again, but not Betty. This created a conflict. Betty turned to me.

"It's up to you, Betty, to decide what we're going to play."

"But it's your house," she stomped her foot on the floor.

"Yes, Betty, but this is your play-hour. You invited Lilli, and now you must also decide what you want us to do."

She literally puffed herself up to master this

difficult situation and resolutely walked up to Lilli. "Okay then, you cook something quickly now, and then all three of us will play Parcheesi." Her decision indicated self-confidence on her part: to be able to make concessions, yet keep an eye to her own interests. From then on everything went smoothly. Betty set up the game, chose the colors, then waited patiently until Lilli had served us porridge with raisins in little bowls.

The Parcheesi game began.

I was curious to see how and whether Betty would follow the rules. Lilli got to throw the dice first. Betty warned, "But we're playing without cheating."

Lilli said, "I never cheat!"

"I won't cheat, either," I put in.

Betty said no more, but her cheeks were red as fire. If she won, everything would be fine, but I feared the worst in case she lost. At first Betty was lucky and threw a lot of sixes. All her men were on the board. It looked good for her. Suddenly Lilli was catching up, sending Betty's men back to "Go" time and again. Fortune was on Lilli's side.

Betty was crushed. The first tears rolled down her cheeks. Yet she kept on playing to the end without cheating. For Betty this was a great accomplishment, indeed. We still had time for another game. I was willing secretly to do everything to help Betty win this game.

She won the game. Again she wrote on the

blackboard "I won once. Lilli won once. And Mrs. Ude always lost."

As the girls said good-bye, their thoughts were obviously already at the skating-rink.

38

"Yes, and now I don't dream at all anymore!"

"Here, a present for you." Betty pressed a glass marble into my hand. "My most beautiful marble. You're glad, aren't you?"

"Very glad, Betty. I'll put it in a special place in my apartment."

"Today we have to hurry," Betty continued, "We've got to play a whole lot."

"You've already decided what we're going to play?"

"I feel like playing with the Sceno-box." She headed straight for the table and began at once. "It's going to be a large farm with meadows, trees and flowers and a big house, with the farmer standing in front of it." The farm was alive with animals—chickens, geese, pigs. For the cow Betty prepared a comfortable stall cushioned with grass and flowers for fodder. A little rabbit came up to the cow and played affectionately with her. It sat on the cow's back and cheerfully rode around the farm. Once the cow went wild and trampled angrily all over the farm. But she soon became calm again. The farmer came to milk her. Betty accompanied this with swishing sounds and then pretended to pour the milk into little baby-bottles. She petted the cow affectionately, lay her on her side, and pointed at her, "That's her belly button. The cow is a mother."

The story went on.

The farmer fed all the animals, and as night came, they all went to sleep. At dawn the rooster crowed on the roof of the farmhouse, the sun rose and all the animals and flowers woke up. "And now another beautiful and peaceful day starts out for them," Betty said at the end. She looked up at me.

"That was lovely, Betty. I like your farm with flowers and trees and the beautiful house, where the farmer takes good care of everything and feeds all the animals, and with the cow who gives milk and even lets the bunny ride on her. You can feel at home on this farm; night is welcome, because you know that the sun will rise again in the morning, bringing a beautiful day for everyone."

Betty was visibly pleased to hear me speak in detail about her beautiful farm.

"And because you like my farm so much, let's leave it set up as it is until next time."

"Yes, let's do that."

The way Betty was looking at me, I sensed that something was bothering her. "Who do I love more, my Mommy or you?" Her expression told me that a certain anxiety had prompted her question and that she expected a definite answer. She repeated, "Who do I love more, my Mommy or you?"

"I told you before, Betty, your strength to love

grows as you begin to love more and more people. The more people you love, the more you can love one person. And although you love others and me, you will love your Mommy even more. That's how love works."

Whenever an answer goes to the heart, silence follows. Betty thought and arrived at the perceptive conclusion: "The more people you love, the less you need to feel afraid."

"That's right, Betty!"

She went on philosophizing, "And when you don't love anyone at all, you're always afraid." With this she ran to the xylophone, sounded the notes, and sang again, "Up here is heaven and down here is hell; up here is peace and down here death; up here is goodness and down here evil."

"Yes, Betty, everything is one, it is all part of life."

"Just like here"—she was turning Peter's candle—"This is the good side and this is the bad one."

"Yes, Betty."

She studied my face and then asked, "Why don't you wear bangs some time?"

"Bangs, like your Mommy's?"

"Oh, well, you better stay the way you are," she decided after a moment of silence." (At the beginning of her therapy Betty twice had anxiously demanded, "Push the hair out of your face!" At the time she had unconsciously been apprehensive of projecting her negative feelings for her mother on me. The fact that she no longer needed to fear such a projection indicated that her unconscious had found a positive image of her mother.) "Tell me," she continued, "why do you always play with me? Why am I coming here, anyway?"

"When you first came to see me, Betty, you often had bad dreams."

"Yes, and now," Betty chimed in, "now I don't dream at all anymore. I wish I could dream something really beautiful some time." She changed the subject again. "In two weeks my Mommy and Daddy, Sebastian and me are going away for a vacation. I can't wait to go. I won't see you for a long time. Who will play with you then?"

"But you know that I'm not alone, Betty. I've already been thinking that you don't need to come to see me so regularly anymore. You need so much time now for other things. What do you think of that?"

"Why don't I do this: when I feel like coming, I'll call you first."

"Let's do it that way, Betty. And next week you'll be coming once more before you go on your big trip."

"I'll write to you," she added as if wanting to comfort me.

Saying good-bye, she kissed me for the first time.

Lisa was already waiting outside. She handed me a large envelope with pictures Betty had drawn at home in the past week (picture 24). Under the bright sun a cow is grazing in a rich meadow, her udder well-rounded with milk. This picture complemented Betty's Sceno-play perfectly. In her unconscious Betty had formed a positive mother image.

Another picture showed a colorful butterfly.

The last picture I pulled out had a big heart on it, framed by many little hearts. Betty apparently drew the picture with much love for her mother:

"Dear Mommy, I am very happy." (picture 25)

39

"But what I'm going to draw for you now, is the most beautiful of all."

Today Betty was coming for the last time before her summer vacation. (And as it turned out later, for the last time as a patient.) She entered beaming with happiness, announcing right away, "Do you know that I'm going away for a long time with my Mommy and Daddy and Sebastian?"

"Yes, I know. We talked about your trip last time."

"Oh, yeah." Betty headed for the swing. "Are you sad that you won't see me for a long time now?"

"Not sad, Betty; I'm happy for you that you will have such a wonderful trip with your family, but I will think of you a lot."

"Yes, you better," she said emphatically, "and so you won't forget, I'll draw a whole bunch for you today."

The next moment she stood at the blackboard with some chalk, ready to start. "First I'm going to draw a long, happy dog story for you. This is the Mama-dog, and this is the Daddy-dog. This is the big sister-dog, this is the little brother-dog."

195

She quickly sketched four figures on the board, then began to relate their story, "The dog-sister loves her dog-brother very much. Playing with him, she often gets him to laugh. Once the little dog-brother gets lost; he is in danger; his sister searches for him. She finds him. Afterward they romp through meadows and forests and find their way back to their dog-parents." She looked at me, grinning, "How did you like my story?"

"I liked it very much, Betty."

"And you won't erase it right away?"

"No, I promise."

"Good, then I'll draw something really beautiful for you on paper."

Eagerly she fetched a drawing-pad and chalk. She drew a large oval shape. "This is an egg." She drew another egg with a little crack at the top. "There's a tiny chick inside, it just pecked at its shell, because it wants to come out." In a third picture she drew a cracked egg shell from which, as she said, the chick had just come out. She looked at me proudly. "How do you like this?"

"I like this just as much as the dog story," I replied and added, "A chick was just born, wasn't it?"

"Yes, the chick has its birthday." Then she went over to the pot of clay, dumped it out, and started to form a gigantic ball. She truly enjoyed herself. Then she rolled the ball under the swing, stood on the board, and gleefully swung herself high up into the air.

"That's a globe," she called, "and I'm flying, flying

way above it." Pushing vigorously, she was able to touch the ceiling with the tips of her toes now and then. "How long have we known each other, Mrs. Ude?" she called down to me.

"How long do you think it is, Betty?"

"It must be very, very long. I don't know how long."

"You weren't in school yet, Betty. You came here before school started. And now you're almost finished with the second grade."

"That long! We've known each other for that long? Then, you're my oldest friend. I haven't known Lilli that long. I didn't meet her until I was in school." The swing died down and she jumped.

"I know what else I'll draw." And squatting on the floor, she drew a sweeping rainbow with all its colors. "How do you like this?" she exclaimed proudly.

"That's beautiful, Betty!"

"Which do you think is the most beautiful of all the pictures I painted today?"

"One picture is as beautiful as the other." She saw how glad I was.

"But what I'm going to draw for you now, is the most beautiful of all. You can hang it up in your livingroom." With quick strokes she drew a self-portrait: a dancing girl in a blue polka dot dress and with long, brown hair (picture 27).

"And how do you like this one?" She asked with joyful pride.

"I like this one best of all, Betty. You couldn't

have given me a more beautiful present."

"Where are you going to put it?"

"Upstairs in my apartment where I can look at it often."

"That's good. And when I come to visit you, you'll show me where you put it."

The hour had flown by.

"Byyye, Mrs. Ude," she said, kissing me, "and have some fun, too."

"Bye, Betty, have a good vacation."

The door closed behind her.

As if she knew that today had been her last hour with me, she poked her head once more around the door. "Byyyyyee!"

"Bye, Betty."

It was easy for her to leave. Happily she dashed off to drive home with Lisa.

A Note from Betty's mother

Two months later I received a large picture of Betty in the mail with a few lines from her mother:

"For this happy smile of your play-child we thank you cordially,

> Yours,
> Barbara and Walter Bonsart"

I placed the photograph of Betty under her drawing of the "Dancing girl." I was happy and relieved—yet at the same time apprehensive. In spite of the success of her therapy, Betty and her parents still had a long, precarious path ahead.

EPILOGUE to the American Edition (late 1976)

Several years later

On a cold November day Betty appeared at my door, holding a violin case. "I wanted to see you again," she said, smiling, obviously delighted at my surprise.

"Oh, Betty!" I exclaimed, hugging her. I was also surprised that she was not really a child any more. She was 12 years old and seemed so grown up.

Immediately she went into the living room. It was clear that she felt as much at home as ever. She knelt at the fireplace and rubbed her hands. "Would you have something hot for me to drink?" she asked.

"So, it is that cold today!"

While she was sipping the hot tea I made for her, her eyes searched the room.

"Everything is as it was," she said. "Here is the old bellows still." She made the blaze roar in the fireplace. Then she started talking about her violin teacher. She said he had moved into my neighborhood and that she would be seeing him once a week. She spoke very enthusiastically about him and said it was so much fun learning to play the violin. I put more wood on the fire and the flames seemed to ignite her memories. "Do you remember, Mrs. Ude, how we always burned the bad ghosts here?"

"Yes, Betty," I answered. "You were so pleased when they disappeared up through the chimney."

"So it was, so it was," she said. "And you always let me play whatever I wanted to play."

"Do you still remember what we played, Betty?" I asked.

She lay down on the floor and stretched out like a cat. "Everything. Everything we played made me happy. And when I was sad, I wanted to play being your baby. Do you remember?" she said, laughing, "I even drank out of the baby bottle. And you carried me or pushed me around in the big chair. I felt like a little baby and that was just beautiful." She jumped to her feet. "Let's go into the playroom!" She immediately sat in the swing. "Do you remember," she began, "always when I came to you I sat first in the swing?" She pointed to the little rocking-horse. "And there you sat. And when I came, I often felt so bad. And we would play together and then it was better."

"You remember all of this, Betty?"

"I can remember everything," she said. "Here, in this flower box I planted onions, do you remember?"

"Yes, Betty, I remember very well."

"And then I always ripped off the roots from the onions, and washed them and peeled them and planted them again. Do you remember that?"

"You remember very well, Betty."

"And when the onions had roots again, I was very pleased."

"I know that was very important for you, Betty."

She wandered through the room. "Everything—everything is just the same as it was."

"Does that make you happy?"

"Oh, yes! I want to remember everything!" She stopped in front of the Kasper theater. "You sat behind here very often, telling me fairy tales."

"What were the fairy tales about?"

She didn't have to search her memory. "A brother and a sister, the fairy tale of the owl, who helped the water nymph to become a human being. And the story of the young maid who made the white gosling yellow by using pollen so it looked the same as the other goslings." I was astonished at how much she remembered.

She sat on the little rocking-horse. "And do you remember," she began, "that once I was very sad. And we played I was a flower, and it was snowing, and I was covered with snow?"

"How did we end that game, Betty?"

"There was no end," she said. "It was just a beautiful play." Then she recalled our game of hide and seek. "You always knew where I hid myself," she said. "But it was *so* wonderful when you looked for me such a long time." She looked at me. "I always had such terrible fears and such bad dreams. Sometimes I called you."

"And how is it now?" I asked her quietly. "Do you still feel anxious and have bad dreams?"

She did not answer right away, thinking over the question. It seemed to me that she was considering her emotional inner balance. I compared this 12-year-old Betty, relaxed and confident, to the little 6-year-old Betty, with the nervous twitching, the drooping eyelid and the shifty glance. All of that was gone.

"I sleep very well," she answered. "I don't feel anxious anymore." She hesitated. "Maybe just now as I remember that anxiety, I am a little afraid—afraid, the dreams would come back. It was a very bad time."

"Yes, it was, Betty. But you helped yourself when it was so very bad. Do you now?"

"Yes, oh, yes, yes!" she cried, jumping up. "When I threw the mud against the wall—that was so great when it splashed against the wall. That was a lot of fun."

"And that was good, too, Betty. One should not hold back feelings, because locking them up makes one anxious."

We went back to the living room. Betty opened her violin case. "Let me play you something on my violin. I'll play a song." Then she became a little silly, giggling, as all girls her age so love to do. "It's a love song." Then before she started to play, her voice dropped. "I have a boy friend. I am in love," she said. "But he doesn't know it yet! I'm going to invite him to my birthday party."

"That sounds good, Betty; it is good to be in love." She giggled, then became serious, concentrating hard, pressing her violin under her chin, carefully tuning it. Finally she stood, composed, and poised like an artist ready to play for a big audience. It was such a joy to look at this beautiful girl. She was able to draw such beautiful sounds from her violin and I thought once more about the little 6-year-old Betty who could only express her anxiety and needs symbolically in paintings. That same creativity in this gifted girl enabled her to play the violin so beautifully. The very sound of her music echoed with the joy of living.

When Betty had been there about an hour she said that she should call her mother and tell her that she would be a little late. The line was busy. "When my mother is on the phone it can take a long time," she said.

"Shall I call her for you, Betty? Then you can be on your way." She agreed.

As we said our goodbyes, Betty asked, "Are you going to California—to Angeles again?

"Yes, Betty," I corrected gently, "to Los Angeles."

"Oh. Los Angeles. What does that mean?"

"That is Spanish and it means, 'the angels.' "

Betty chuckled. "So, then you are flying to the angels. I wouldn't want to be an angel. That's too strenuous, to have to always be good!"

I laughed and put my hands on her shoulders. "I love to see you this way, Betty."

"You will send me a postcard as you did once, with palm trees on it? They grow there, don't they?" I nodded as she pulled the hood of her warm coat over her head and set out on her way home. It was wonderful. She could now express the normal concerns of a normal girl in a normal way and be as outgoing and spontaneous as any child.

Figure 1: Strangled deadman

Figure 2: Dismembered deadman

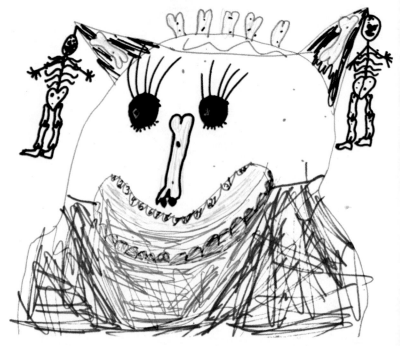

Figure 3: Ghost with two child skeletons

Figure 4: Crocodiles with child skeletons

Figure 5: Vulture with children

Figure 6: "Large ghost bites into child's blood"

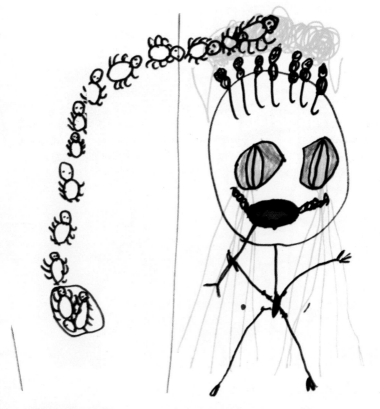

Figure 7: Girl's head with mice and spiders

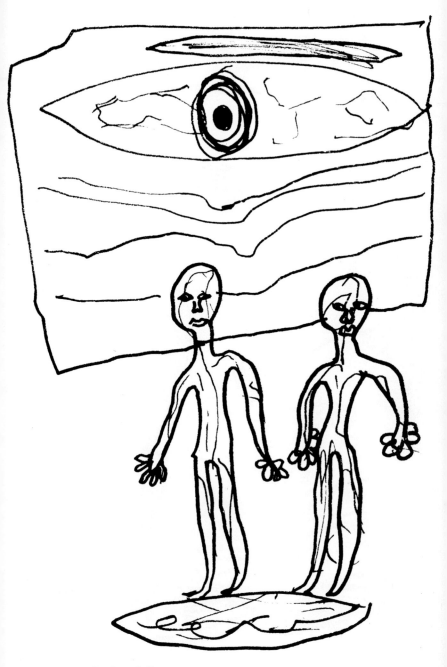

Figure 8: Broken dolls

Figure 9: Embryo

Figure 10: Indian girl on the cross

Figure 11: Portrait of a woman

Figure 12: Rat in the mind

Figure 13: Sun with evil fingers

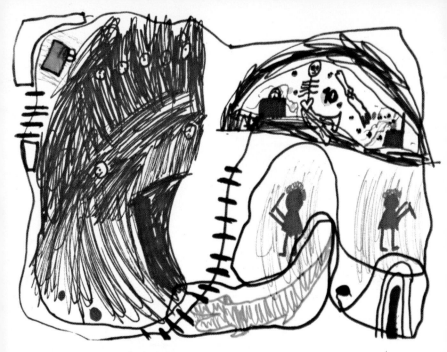

Figure 14: Gorgonian head

Figure 15: Dinosaur

Figure 16: Mute school-girl

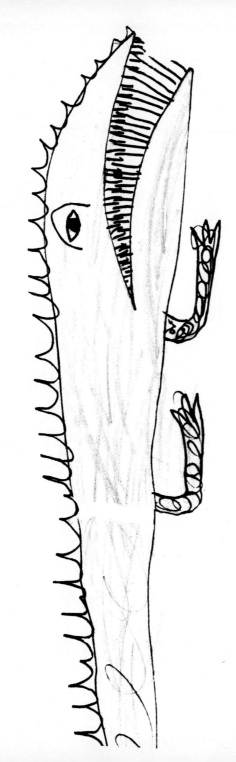

Figure 18: Giant crocodile

Figure 19: Female dog

Figure 20: Girl with penis—Ghost in the bathroom

Figure 21: Birth and dancing death

Figure 22: Witches

Figure 23: Heart—Doctor (Arzt)

Figure 24: Cow in the meadow

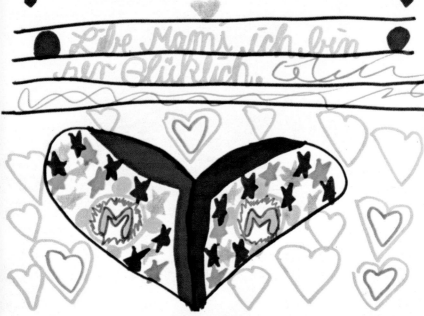

Figure 25: A heart for Mommy (Dear Mommy, I am verry happy)

Figure 26: Dancing girl

DISCARD